Spain's Transition
to Democracy

Studies of the Research Institute on
International Change, Columbia University

Seweryn Bialer, Series Editor

About the Book and Author

After the death of longtime dictator Generalissimo Franco in 1975, King Juan Carlos acted decisively to institute a dramatic change in Spanish politics. By appointing an unknown Christian democrat, Adolfo Suarez, as prime minister, the king paved the way for the transformation of Spain from an authoritarian regime to a liberal democracy. Central to this singular transition was the formulation of the new Spanish constitution, an unusual process of political give and take. Dr. Bonime-Blanc examines the evolutionary phases of the constitution-making process, describing the conflicts, maneuvers, and compromises of the principal political players involved. Analyzing the negotiations and their constitutional results, she pinpoints the factors that make a successful transition to democracy possible. In her closing chapter, the author illustrates the lessons of the Spanish case and their practical implications for future transitions to democracy.

Andrea Bonime-Blanc is a lawyer at the New York office of the international law firm of Cleary, Gottlieb, Steen & Hamilton. She is also a research associate with the Research Institute on International Change, Columbia University, and a member of the Council on Foreign Relations.

Spain's Transition to Democracy

The Politics of Constitution-making

Andrea Bonime-Blanc

Westview Press / Boulder and London

Studies of the Research Institute on International Change, Columbia University

This Westview softcover edition is printed on acid-free paper and bound in softcovers that carry the highest rating of the National Association of State Textbook Administrators, in consultation with the Association of American Publishers and the Book Manufacturers' Institute.

Copyright © 1987 by Westview Press, Inc.

Published in 1987 in the United States of America by Westview Press, Inc.; Frederick A. Praeger, Publisher; 5500 Central Avenue, Boulder, Colorado 80301

Library of Congress Cataloging-in-Publication Data
Bonime-Blanc, Andrea
  Spain's transition to democracy.
  (Studies of the Research Institute on International
Change, Columbia University)
  Bibliography: p.
  Includes index.
  1. Spain—Constitutional history. I. Title.
II. Series.
LAW   342.46   85-31541
ISBN 0-8133-7147-3   344.602

Composition for this book was created by conversion of the author's word-processor disks. This book was produced without formal editing by the publisher.

Printed and bound in the United States of America

∞ The paper used in this publication meets the requirements of the American National
   Standard for Permanence of Paper for Printed Library Materials Z39.48-1984.

6   5   4   3   2   1

For my husband and my mother

Contents

Tables and Figures

Figures

Acknowledgments

I am grateful to many for the comments and encouragement provided during the completion of this book. I am especially thankful to Dr. Seweryn Bialer, who, as my doctoral adviser at Columbia University, expressed an early interest in my ideas about transitions to democracy. Dr. Bialer and the Research Institute on International Change at Columbia University have been invaluable sources of encouragement since the inception of this work. I owe a deep debt of gratitude to Professor Juan J. Linz and his wife, whose hospitality, generosity with source materials and constructive criticism were central to the writing of this book. I have also benefited greatly from the comments, guidance and suggestions of Professors Douglas A. Chalmers, John N. Hazard, Kenneth Maxwell, Glenda Rosenthal and Giovanni Sartori. Special thanks go to Dr. Zbigniew Brzezinski, with whom I studied and worked at Columbia, and former Ambassador Richard N. Gardner, whose seminars I attended at Columbia's Law School, for their policy-oriented approach to the study of politics. I believe that such an approach is fundamental to the development of political science as a discipline and have tried in this volume to incorporate aspects of this approach. There is a final group of individuals without whose support this book would not have been possible. I thank my friend, Marjean Knokey, for all her help at the Research Institute on International Change since early 1981. I am very grateful to Annette Matteo for enduring the hardship of typing (and retyping) the many tables in this book without ever losing her smile. Finally, I wish to thank my ever-patient and supportive editor at Westview, Susan McEachern, for prodding me to go the extra mile in completing this volume.

Andrea Bonime-Blanc

Acronyms

AP	Popular Alliance/Alianza Popular
CC	Catalan Convergence/Convergencia Catalana
CCOO	Workers Commissions/Comisiones Obreras
CDS	Party of the Social Democratic Center (Portugal)
CDU/CSU	Christian Democratic Party/Coalition (West Germany)
DC	Christian Democrats (Italy)
EE	Basque Left/Euskadi Esquerra/Euzkadiko Ezkerra
EEC	European Economic Community
ETA	Euzkadi ta Azkatasuna
FDP	Free Democratic Party (West Germany)
FN	New Force/Fuerza Nueva
HB	Popular Unity/Herri Batasuna
LCR	Revolutionary Communist League/Liga Revolucionaria Comunista
MC	Catalan Minority/Minoria Catalana
NATO	North Atlantic Treaty Organization
PCE	Spanish Communist Party/Partido Comunista Español
PCI	Italian Communist Party
PCP	Portuguese Communist Party
PNV	Basque National Party/Partido Nacional Vasco
PPD	People's Democratic Party (Portugal)
PS	Socialist Party (Portugal)
PSOE	Spanish Socialist Workers Party/Partido Socialista Obrero Español
PSP	Popular Socialist Party/Partido Socialista Popular
PSUC	Unified Socialist Party of Catalonia/Partido Socialista Unificado Catalan
PTE	Spanish Workers Party/Partido del Trabajo Español
SPD	Social Democratic Party (West Germany)
UCD	Union of the Democratic Center/Union del Centro Democratico
UGT	General Workers Union/Union General del Trabajo

Introduction

Constitutions, constitution-making and transitions from authoritarianism to democracy are rarely studied. Since constitutions are often dismissed as impractical symbols, the study of constitution-making processes would appear to be a purposeless pursuit. A handful of observers feel differently, however, and have demonstrated the utility of understanding a nation's constitution.[1] Transitions to democracy are another neglected topic. Transitions from authoritarian to democratic regimes, in particular, have been rare and, until the early 1970s in Southern Europe, not very recent.

Sketchy journalistic accounts have been quick to emerge, but analytical and policy-oriented studies have been few and far between. Most of these have been specialized studies of electoral patterns, elite behavior and the like. Overall attempts to grasp the dynamics of an entire transition are nowhere to be found. This paucity of material may be explained by the need to have monographic material before one can engage in a comprehensive study. On the other hand, an excuse for this dearth of material is that it is difficult (and perhaps unscholarly) to construct a general theory of transitions to democracy because each transition is unique. However, the events that in the last decade have swept the globe—first in Southern Europe, then in Latin America, and, in 1986, in Haiti and the Philippines—have made these excuses invalid.

A principal goal of this book is to show how vitally important the transitionary constitution-making process is to the success of democratization. In addition, the long neglected subjects of constitutions and constitution-making are reintroduced into the study of politics. Whether or not a constitution accurately reflects reality, it is nevertheless a useful tool with which to understand a political system. When it does mirror reality, a constitution operates as a roadmap displaying the institutional and political landscape of a nation.

Serious questions arise, however, when a constitution does not accurately reflect such realities. To understand the nature of a regime, it is important to understand why its constitution clashes with reality and what the alternative political arrangements are. The constitution provides a yardstick with which to do this.

Constitution-making during a transition to democracy is a pre-constitutional process that does not exist within a particular regime. It is rather a development that fills an inter-regime vacuum. Such a process does not reflect the same kinds of political realities that an effective constitution does. Constitution-making reveals in a microcosm the political climate of the larger polity during the transition. Therein lies its significance.

It is now useful to preview some of the more important issues raised in this book. Does reform within an authoritarian regime help sow the seeds for a transition to democracy or do other factors, such as the pressure of an organized opposition, better explain such an outcome? Are there several types of "turning points" toward democratization and, if so, is a particular type of turning point related to a particular type of transition? If ideology plays a role in the constitution-making process, what is its practical impact? What mechanisms, if any, do constitution-makers devise to resolve disputes and how satisfactory are such devices in light of the political, social and economic needs of a nation?

Plan and Overview

Chapter 1 of Part 1 is an introduction to the general topic of constitution-making during transitions to democracy. Chapter 2 examines Spain's turning point toward democratization, exploring how the political elites handled the critical choice between continuity, reform and "ruptura."

In Part 2, Spain's constitution-making process is examined in depth. Chapter 3 describes the official or "technical" phases of the process and surveys the political actors involved. In Chapter 4, the political composition and strategies of the constitution-makers' shifting coalitions are traced and the more significant political (rather than "technical") phases of the process are dissected. Chapters 5 and 6 discuss the contents of the new constitutional document by analyzing its "political" and "sociogovernmental" formulas.

In Part 3, Chapter 7 briefly compares Spain's experience to that of several other European nations, and a concluding chapter offers a policy oriented framework for the study and practice of constitution-making during transitions to democracy.

Notes

1. See, e.g., S. E. Finer, ed., *Five Constitutions* (Sussex, N.J.: Harvester Press/ Humanities Press, 1979).

Part 1

1

Constitutions, Constitution-making and Transitions from Authoritarian to Democratic Regimes

During the mid–1970s, the world witnessed a rebirth of experiments in democratization. Within three years, regime transformations in Greece, Portugal and Spain changed the political face of southern Europe. An historically unusual development—transitions from authoritarian to democratic regimes—evolved in each of these nations. Each transition developed without foreign intervention or widespread domestic instability. In the mid–1980s, a resurgence of such experiments in democratization in Latin America, the Caribbean and the Philippines has made such transitions a most fascinating political development to study.

Transitions from Authoritarian to Democratic Regimes: A Preliminary Framework

A transition from authoritarianism to democracy is a type of political change on par, in its consequences, with a revolution, a civil war or a coup d'etat. To understand such a transition, one must first understand the nature of the regimes the transition is evolving from and to. In his valuable work on authoritarianism, Juan J. Linz provides a useful definition of authoritarian regimes:

> Authoritarian regimes are political systems with limited, not responsible, political pluralism; without elaborate and guiding ideology (but with distinctive mentalities); without intensive or extensive political mobilization . . . and in which a leader (or occasionally a small group) exercises power within formally ill-defined limits but actually quite predictable ones.[1]

5

By utilizing contrasting concepts, one can turn Linz's definition of authoritarian regimes into a useful definition of democratic regimes: Democratic regimes are political systems with mostly unrestricted and responsible political pluralism; with a variety of political ideologies and mentalities; with some political mobilization and participation possible through political parties; and in which a leader(s) exercises power within formally well defined limits (constitutional ones) that are normally quite predictable.

Although he characterizes democracy as defying definition, Robert Dahl's discussion of democracy is also worth mentioning. Democracies (or polyarchies, as Dahl designates them) are regimes with a substantial amount of liberalization (defined as public contestation or political competition) and inclusiveness (defined as participation).[2] Using Dahl's concepts, one can in turn characterize an authoritarian system as one with a minimal amount of liberalization (defined as political mono-polization and non-contestation) and exclusiveness (defined as non-participation).

Finally, while an authoritarian regime's leader may be characterized as a-constitutional, or abusive of constitutional limitations (assuming there are any), a democratic executive has usually well defined powers limited not only by other constitutionally sanctioned powers (the judiciary and the legislative) but also by constitutionally predictable limits (a specific term in office, electoral limitations, etc.).

What Is a "Transition to Democracy"?

If the authoritarian regime is the starting point and the democratic regime is the end-point of the transition, the transition may be preliminarily defined as an evolutionary period of reform coupled with regime change. Such a period of reform and regime change may contain two or more of the following developments: (1) the pluralization and mobilization of society from below; (2) the liberalization of socioeconomic policies; (3) the constitutionalization of political activity; and (4) the liberalization and possible democratization of the bureaucracy. A transition is an evolution between regimes that is neither a violent revolutionary change of regimes nor a set of piecemeal reforms within the same regime.

Social Pluralization and Mobilization. The non-governmentally sponsored mobilization of society from below into independent social, political and economic groups is a potentially crucial factor for the success of a transition. These groups' independence is evident in both their grassroots origins and their autonomy from governmental control.

This pluralization may be broad, well organized and long lasting if the autonomous groups (labor, student, religious, political) are capable of maintaining their existence under the authoritarian regime. Short-term pluralization involves a more unexpected and erratic appearance and disappearance of groups challenging the authoritarian system. The presence of either type of pluralization may be a crucial prerequisite to a transitionary turning point. The likelihood of reaching such a turning point or of bloody failure is greatest in the case of long-term pluralization. Witness the case of Spain in the 1970s as an example of success and the case of contemporary South Africa as an ongoing example of bloody failure.

The likelihood of failure to reach the transitionary turning point (whether violent or not) is greater in cases of short-term pluralization as there is no sustained anti-authoritarian effort. Haiti in the 1960s and 1970s, especially when Baby Doc Duvalier succeeded Papa Doc Duvalier, represented a case of such a failure. Haiti in 1986, however, demonstrates that short-term pluralization can work to create a transitionary turning point. Whether reaching such a turning point successfully translates into an actual transition to democracy is a separate question.

The Liberalization of Socioeconomic Policy. This development involves the implementation of social and economic policy reforms. Authoritarian policies are characterized by greater control from above, ideological content and the subordination of societal needs to governmental goals. Liberalized policies are based on broader views, are generally less ideological and are subject to some input from below.

Socioeconomic policy liberalization may take place under the authoritarian regime only if its elite (or a segment thereof) recognizes pluralization and, as a consequence, becomes involved in reform. This authoritarian liberalization of policy may indeed act as a double sword. While aiming to quell social discontent, reform may also whet the appetite of those who have been oppressed for so long. Socioeconomic policy liberalization is, however, much more likely to take place once the authoritarian regime has broken down and the transitionary turning point has been reached.

The Constitutionalization of Political Activity. The constitutionalization of political activity consists of the democratic reordering and restructuring of political rules and institutions. Such democratic mainstays as regular elections, freedom of association, the separation of governmental powers and the guaranteeing of individual liberties are reintegrated into the mainstream of the polity.

Such a reorganization of political rules and institutions requires both an elite decision-making phase and an implementation phase. The decision-making phase is the constitution-making process per se wherein the constitution-makers hammer out the shape of the constitutional document. The implementation phase follows the approval and adoption of the new constitution and consists of the practical translation of constitutional theory into political action.

The Liberalization and Democratization of the Bureaucracy. Both the liberalization and the democratization of the bureaucracy are rarer developments which may or may not take place during or immediately after the transition. A complete liberalization and democratization of decision-making patterns within a bureaucracy would take place along four dimensions:

1. From responsibility concentrated in one individual to vesting it in a procedure regulating a shared authority,
2. From control of dissidence by arbitrary coercion to coercion regulated by norms and law,
3. From a restricted to a pluralist participation in policy making, and
4. From a distorted to an open flow of information.[3]

While items 1, 2 and 4 are necessary for an overall transition to democracy to take place, such developments do not automatically take place within existing (authoritarian) bureaucratic structures. The transitionary elite must make conscious decisions concerning the bureaucracy. They can either abolish authoritarian bureaucratic structures or implement the above three liberalizing changes within such structures.

The transitionary elite (or first legitimately elected democratic elite) may go one step further, however. They can attempt to implement item 3—subjecting the bureaucracy to a pluralistic input similar to the pluralistic participation of society in the larger political arena.

Transitions and Revolutions

As suggested earlier, the transition refers to a period of reformist change between regimes—not to a change of government within the same constitutional framework nor to a revolutionary transformation. Some of the crucial differences between transitions and revolutions are the following:

1. Although transitions may have *violent situations*, they do not involve, as do revolutions, prolonged or intensely violent struggles for power comprising the whole or large sections of society.
2. In transitions, changes in the composition of governmental elites are either (a) *incremental*, insofar as elites from the previous regime may stay in positions of power while new (previously excluded) elites become part of the establishment or (b) *substitutive*, in that

although previously governmental elites no longer occupy positions of power, and new (previously excluded) elites take their place, the former are not purged or eliminated as would former elites in the case of revolutions.

3. The architects and participants of a transitionary process do not aim at total transformation of economics, society, politics and ideology as do revolutionaries. The transitionary elites instead seek a qualitative and incremental reform accompanied by regime change.

4. Finally, a transition may often preempt what had or could have become a revolutionary situation.

Constitutions and Constitution-making

Authoritarian leaders often support their actions with ambiguous legal documents masquerading as constitutions. Generalissimo Francisco Franco's Fundamental Laws and Philippine President Ferdinand Marcos' Decrees are examples of such authoritarian misuse of the constitutional form. In Spain, seven basic laws were passed intermittently over a period of nearly thirty years. These laws often overlapped and never provided a coherent constitutional framework for the practice of politics under Franco.

Constitutions are often used as well in totalitarian regimes. Following Linz's definition, these are regimes with a single power center, an exclusive, autonomous and elaborate ideology and single party popular mobilization from above. These regimes also frequently use terror as a policy of repression.[4] How is one to reconcile the human rights, popular participation and power limitation clauses in such constitutions with these regimes' totalitarian practices?

In view of the widespread uses and abuses of the constitutional form, let us turn to a brief discussion of constitutions. It is essential to understand what a constitution is in order to grasp what makes it a uniquely democratic tool rather than an authoritarian or totalitarian device. If during a constitution-making process non-democratic principles are introduced and incorporated into the new document, not only is the transition threatened but so is the likelihood of a democratic regime resulting from such a process.

Defining a Constitution

Most people (especially Americans) would first think of the protection of individual liberties as the primary purpose of a constitution. Many would also agree that a constitution is some kind of official legal

document which is *supposed* to describe the permissible scope and limits
of governmental power. In one of the few good books on the subject,
S. E. Finer's *Five Constitutions*, the following definition of constitution
is offered:

> Constitutions are codes of rules which aspire to regulate the allocation
> of functions, powers and duties among the various agencies and officers
> of government, and define the relationships between these and the public.[5]

Carl Friedrich provides a more succinct definition in *Constitutional
Government and Democracy* where he describes a constitution as "effective regularized restraint."[6] Based on such a notion of restraint,
Friedrich classifies regimes on a continuum from unconstitutional (regimes lacking restraint) and actual governments (those having some
restraint) to constitutional governments (those with complete restraint).

An observer of constitutions in third world nations, B. O. Nwabueze
in *Constitutionalism in the Emergent States*, sees these documents as
limiters of arbitrary power, requiring the consent of the governed and
applying "predetermined rules" on government. They are also filled
with "lofty declarations," commanding the "loyalty, obedience and
confidence of the people" while guaranteeing human rights.[7]

Giovanni Sartori provides an even more direct definition, describing
a constitution as a "technique of liberty."[8] Sartori's words capture the
essence of a constitution. At its best a constitution is an unambiguous
technical document which shows how political power is limited and
how individual and societal rights are protected. Regimes which in
practice live up to these techniques of liberty are democracies. Authoritarian and totalitarian regimes display varying degrees of characteristics antithetical to the principles of democracy—political power is
not limited or checked and individual liberties are not properly protected.
Hence the inherently democratic nature of a constitution.

The extent to which a constitutional document departs in practice
from what it conveys in words is an important yardstick with which
to classify and distinguish constitutions. On this basis, Karl Loewenstein
has provided a useful typology of constitutions. *Normative* constitutions
are those that in practice are fully activated and effective. *Nominal*
constitutions may be legally valid but are not implemented—they are
unexecuted blueprints. Finally, the *semantic* constitution is used for
"legalizing, stabilizing and perpetuating an existing configuration of
power (but) cannot serve as the procedural frame for the competitive
power elements." While *normative* constitutions are typical of western
democracies, *semantic* ones may be found in both totalitarian and
authoritarian regimes. *Nominal* constitutions are common in nations

where a western constitution "is implemented into a colonial and/or agrarian-feudal social structure."[9]

Sartori offers another classification of constitutions. He distinguishes between *nominal, real* and *façade* constitutions depending on whether they are unexecuted blueprints, effectively implemented documents or mere devices behind which lurk repressive regimes.[10] Finer, on the other hand, fits constitutions along a continuum from *entirely realistic description* to *unrealistic fiction.* Between these necessarily abstract extremes, Finer differentiates the more useful categories of *entirely* or *largely non-fictive* constitutions (those found in working democracies) and *partially non-fictive* constitutions such as the current Soviet constitution.[11]

Constitutions and Regimes

These classifications and definitions lead us to several observations about constitutions and what makes them "democratic." Constitutions can and do exist in every type of regime—from the most totalitarian to the most democratic. But each type of regime uses or abuses its constitution according to the existing power structures and practices. Each regime would claim to have a *real* constitution, i.e., one which the regime fully implements. The totalitarian regime views its constitution as a legitimator of its rule and a stabilizer of its society. Such a regime nevertheless uses its constitution as a façade behind which it exercises a political power very different from that wielded in a democracy. For example, Article 125 of the Constitution of the Union of Soviet Socialist Republics of 1936 guarantees freedom of speech, freedom of the press, freedom of assembly and rallies and freedom of street processions and demonstrations. This provision was enacted during Stalin's massive purge and extermination of his own people in the late 1930s. Need one say more?

When an authoritarian regime happens to have some form of constitutional document, it uses it to claim legitimacy and legality. The authoritarian "constitution" is usually a poorly organized collection of decrees filled with empty rhetoric. A cursory comparison of constitutional claims and human rights practices in any authoritarian regime (Salazar's Portugal, Franco's Spain, Marcos' Philippines, Pinochet's Chile, and so on) dramatically proves the *nominal* or *semantic* nature of such constitutions.

What, then, makes a constitution simultaneously *real* and *normative, largely non-fictive* and therefore democratic? One can say that a constitution is *real* and democratic when its written guarantees are actual practices. Such a translation of theory into practice would entail the realization of a number of basic democratic tenets. The institutions described in the constitution actually exist and function in their constitutionally prescribed form. The political timetables delineated in the constitution (for elections and the like) are religiously observed. Abuses of constitutional norms do not go unpunished and are dealt with strictly by law. Human rights, individual and societal, are not widely violated, and when they are, the state takes protective and prosecutorial steps against such violations. These human rights are in turn comprehensive. Some form of separation of powers or system of checks and balances exists to prevent the possibilities of political inbalance and arbitrary power.

The only type of regime that fully follows these constitutional guidelines is a democracy. Only democracies have *real* and *normative* constitutions of *largely non-fictive* quality. It is their departure in practice from the constitutionally proclaimed norms that render authoritarian and totalitarian constitutions *partially non-fictive* or *semantic*. While differences between theory and practice are also possible in democracies, they tend to be less frequent or do not go unnoticed for long. If such departures occur frequently and go unheeded, however, they may be signs that the democratic character of the regime is waning.

A distinction should also be made between a democratic regime with a *largely non-fictive* constitution and one with a *partially fictive* constitution. Democratic regimes with *largely non-fictive* constitutions follow the limits of the constitution closely in practice. Such is the case in most western democracies. Democratic regimes that have *partially fictive* constitutions follow democratic practices to the extent that the constitutional provisions are current and implementable. Parts of such constitutions, however, are obsolete and unreformed. Particular constitutional provisions can no longer be applied to changing and emerging political realities. The amendments to the United States Constitution have helped keep that document practical and updated.

Finally, a formally democratic regime may also abuse its constitutional tenets. In such cases, the regime, while considered democratic in theory, has lost some of its democratic character in deed. The regime is violating the constitution in some significant way and may be evolving into some form of authoritarianism. For example, presidential powers abused in the latter years of the Weimar Republic were a crucial contributor to the advent of Hitler, the demise of democracy and imposition of totalitarianism in Germany.

The Constitution-making Process: A Preliminary Discussion

The constitution-making process is one of the major activities of a transition to democracy. No political group, party or figure can fully avoid personal or ideological involvement in the issues raised during such a period. Everyone—the public and the politicians—knows that the constitution is the legitimator of democracy. It represents *the* democratic prerequisite without which no democracy exists.

Constitution-making is at once the most varied and the most concentrated form of political activity during the transition. In it, political maneuvering, bargaining and negotiating takes place and the political positions, agreements and disagreements between groups and leaders come to the fore. How the constitution drafters handle these issues may tell us crucial things about the transition and about the regime it leads up to. The discrepancies between the words agreed to in the constitution and the political reality that emerges may point to potentially serious future conflicts. The general character of both the process and its outcome may reveal clues about the new regime's potential for stability or instability.

If a constitution is a set of norms and principles limiting political power and protecting individual rights, what is constitution-making? It is a policy-making process in which political elites decide on the limits and practices of the new government and regime (the "political formula"), and on the rights and duties of its citizens (the "sociogovernmental formula"). Constitution-making at its best is a comprehensive attempt at social and political problem solving. Constitution-making during a transition to democracy consists of a momentous set of decisions that may very well affect the viability of the emerging regime. The form that constitution-making takes may also reveal the shape of future domestic political relations.

Three types of constitution-making may be preliminarily distinguished: the consensual, the dissensual and the stillborn. Consensual constitution-making takes place when most (if not all) major political groups participate in the drafting of the constitution. Agreements are reached through compromise, the avoidance of dogmatic solutions and by upholding the notion of political responsibility throughout the process. Because of this compromise, the constitutional text often contains ambiguously written articles. While this ambiguity often irritates one or more political parties, none of them fully opposes the entire text and most of them support it. Spain in the 1970s is the prototype of this kind of constitution-making process.

Dissensual constitution-making is a process in which not all political actors participate, dogmatic solutions prevail and problems are often unresolved or resolved irresponsibly. Agreements are difficult to reach, and if reached, frequently exclude the views of one or more major political parties. The resulting constitutional text is one that poses a potential threat to the stability of the new political system. Such a dissensually created constitution contains solutions satisfactory only to the dominant political force. Spain in the early 1930s exemplified this type of constitution-making process.

Stillborn constitution-making is a process that fails prior to approval and implementation. An example of such a case was the stillborn French constitution rejected by the French electorate on May 5, 1986. Polarized political coalitions contributed to the unacceptable constitutional results of that process. The French constitution-makers regrouped and drafted a second constitution accepted by the electorate on October 13, 1986.[12]

During the constitution-making process, the constitution-makers address two major clusters of decisions, one regarding the shape, limits and functioning of the new government (the political formula) and the other entailing the relationship between government and society and government and the individual (the sociogovernmental formula). A subordinate aspect of this inquiry involves the setting of an agenda for political action. Setting such an agenda means recognizing and addressing the crucial national problems of the day and including their consideration in the constitutional talks. It also means prioritizing these issues properly giving the most urgent issues precedence over the less critical ones. If it is not appropriate to include a particular problem in the constitutional talks or in the resulting constitution, suitable arrangements must be made for the extra- or post-constitutional handling of the issue.

Conclusion

This brief discussion has tried to highlight the fact that regimes and constitutions are definitely interrelated. Fundamental texts, moreover, are never lifeless documents. A constitution can always tell us something about the regime within which it exists. When the regime abides by its constitution, the document helps to perpetuate those realities and serves as a useful guide for political life. When a regime does not follow its constitutional precepts, the fundamental text can still serve as a guide in an inquiry into why differences exist between political theory and reality.

In light of the interrelationship between regimes and constitutions, the analysis of the constitution-making process during a transition to democracy becomes an even more intriguing task. Such a study involves capturing an incredibly fluid political situation where neither a regime nor a constitution exists. If the transition succeeds, it will culminate in the creation of both a new regime and a new constitution.

Notes

1. Juan J. Linz, "An Authoritarian Regime: Spain," in *Mass Politics*, eds., Erik Allardt and Stein Rokkan (New York, N.Y.: Free Press, 1970), p. 255.

2. Robert A. Dahl, *Polyarchy: Participation and Opposition* (New Haven, Connecticut: Yale University Press, 1971), pp. 1–9.

3. Douglas A. Chalmers and Craig Robinson, "Why Power Contenders Choose Liberalization Perspectives from Latin America," paper delivered at the American Political Science Association Annual Meeting, 1980, Washington, D.C., p. 8.

4. Juan J. Linz, "Totalitarian and Authoritarian Regimes," in *Handbook of Political Science*, Volume III, Fred Greenstein and Nelson Polsby, eds., (Reading, Massachusetts: Addison Wesley, 1975), pp. 175–412.

5. S. E. Finer, ed. *Five Constitutions* (Sussex, N.J.: The Harvester Press/ Humanities Press, 1979), p. 15.

6. Carl J. Friederich, *Constitutional Government and Democracy: Theory and Practice in Europe and Latin America* (Boston, Mass.: Little, Brown & Co., 1941), pp. 121 ff. Also see his more recent work on the subject: *Limited Government: A Comparison* (Englewood Cliffs, N.J.: Prentice-Hall, 1974).

7. B. O. Nwabueze, *Constitutionalism in the Emergent States* (London: C. Hurst & Co., 1973), pp. 1–4.

8. Giovanni Sartori, "Constitutionalism: A Preliminary Discussion," *American Political Science Review*, Volume LVI, No. 4 (December 1962), p. 862.

9. Karl Loewenstein, "Reflections on the Value of Constitutions in Our Revolutionary Age," in *Constitutions and Constitutional Trends Since World War II*, ed., Arnold J. Zurcher (New York, N.Y.: New York University Press, 1951), pp. 205–206.

10. Sartori, p. 862.

11. Finer, pp. 16–20.

12. Ronald Tiersky, "Alliance Politics and Revolutionary Pretensions," in *Communism in Italy and France,* Donald L.M. Blackmer and Sidney Tarrow, eds. (Princeton, N.J.: Princeton University Press, 1975), pp. 430–431.

2

The Spanish Setting

Spain's turning point toward democratization occurred shortly after Franco's death in 1975. Sociopolitical pluralization and the conscious choice of democratization by authoritarian elites were among the principal factors contributing to the success of such a turning point. This chapter explores some of those crucial social and political trends without which the Spanish transition to democracy may not have been possible.

The Authoritarian Regime

Pluralization Under the Authoritarian Regime

Juan J. Linz offers a useful typology of oppositions to and under an authoritarian regime. He begins with a distinction between "opponents within" and opponents "outside the system" and then provides the following classification:

1. The *Semiopposition* are "those groups that are not dominant or represented in the governing group but that are willing to participate in power without fundamentally challenging the regime." There are three types of *Semiopposition*: (a) groups advocating different emphases in policy; (b) dissidents within the elite "favoring different long run policies;" and, (c) dissidents among those initially identified with the system but not participating in its establishment. The pre-Franco monarchist "Carlists" and the far-right political quasi-party, "Fuerza Nueva" or New Force, were among these groups in Spain.

2. The *Alegal Opposition* "aims at basic change in the regime and in its political institutions and to a large extent a basic change in the social and economic structure" but is reluctant or unable to use illegal means. Many such groups existed in Spain by the

early 1970s. Among these were university student groups, liberal clergymen and informal pro-democratic political groups.
3. The *Illegal Opposition* includes those groups the authoritarian regime officially bans or persecutes and which in the case of authoritarian Spain included the communist and socialist parties and their respective labor unions, the "Comisiones Obreras" (Workers Commissions or "CCOO") and the "Union General del Trabajo" (General Work Union or "UGT").[1]

The Authoritarian Regime and Reform

How does the authoritarian regime react to this social and political pluralization? Can it stem the tide of social demand for reform? Or does it try to satisfy some of these demands? The authoritarian regime has several options. It can refuse to recognize pluralization and choose actively to suppress it. The regime may otherwise ignore these demands by neither suppressing nor responding to them. The regime may react, however, by liberalizing specific policies without implementing general reform nor officially recognizing social or political groups. Finally, the authoritarian regime may do the unexpected and implement an overall policy of reform and democratization.

In the latter years of his rule, Franco made a somewhat feeble attempt at following the third option of piecemeal reform. Carlos Arias Navarro, the first prime minister of the post-Franco era, tried to maintain this course. It was King Juan Carlos, however, who took the decisive first step toward generalized reform and democratization when he dismissed Arias Navarro and appointed Adolfo Suarez as prime minister.

A Brief Review of Franco's Record on Reform

Franco and his ministers first recognized the need to institute economic reforms in the early 1950s when the consequences of Franco's post-civil war policies of economic autarky and isolationism proved too costly. While such policies recognized the need to improve desperate economic conditions, they were initiated solely at the governmental level and were not prompted by widespread or well-organized sociopolitical pressures.

Over the next decade (from the mid–1950s to mid–1960s) some pluralization evolved through the formation of illegal labor movements and political, student and liberal Catholic groups. The authoritarian regime, especially in the area of labor policy, began to feel increasing social pressures and demands. Its responses, throughout the 1960s, were a mix of piecemeal policy reform and overall repression.

By the mid–1960s, new political factors emerged within the authoritarian regime. A limited number of governmental elites became interested in reforming the political system. The extent of this interest never became clear nor did it translate into regularized effective action. From among the ranks of these pro-reform Francoists, however, emerged politicians who would compete in post-Franco democratic politics. Among those who would span both authoritarian and democratic politics were Manuel Fraga Iribarne, a minister under Franco and the leader of the Popular Alliance (a right wing party founded in 1976) and Adolfo Suarez, a Franco bureaucrat and the first democratically elected prime minister in post-Franco Spain.

As he grew older, even Franco realized the need for some reform. His "reform," however, was intended to perpetuate the system he created, not change it. In Linz's terminology, an authoritarian regime is one which has "ill-defined limits." Franco's "ill-defined limits" were embodied in his "Leyes Fundamentales" or Fundamental Laws. Six of these laws were promulgated over a period of twenty years. Franco tried to impose some quasi-constitutional structure on these unrelated laws in 1967 by passing the Seventh Fundamental Law. The leader sought to cloak his system with "democratic" legitimacy by designating his system one of "Organic Democracy." The result, as one author has aptly put it, was one of "façade democracy."[2]

Briefly stated, Franco's seven fundamental laws were the following:

1. The Labor Charter of March 9, 1938 as modified on January 10, 1967.
2. The Law of the Cortes of July 7, 1942 as modified on March 9, 1946 and January 10, 1967.
3. The Charter of the Spanish People of July 17, 1945 as modified on January 10, 1967.
4. The Law on the Referendum of October 22, 1945.
5. The Law on Succession of July 7, 1945 as modified on January 10, 1967.
6. The Law on the Principles of the National Movement of May 15, 1958.
7. The Organic Law of the State of January 10, 1967.[3]

Franco's "political reform" went further than he had envisioned. Important developments with a profound impact on the demise of the authoritarian system followed the 1967 "reforms." Little did Franco suspect that he had laid down crucial seeds for a "legal" transition to democracy by designating Prince Juan Carlos de Borbon y Borbon his successor as Head of State, and General Carrero Blanco his first Head of Government (until then Franco had held both titles). Franco had personally supervised the Prince's rearing and education and trusted him implicitly as an ideal successor. The future King, however, turned out to be the opposite of Franco's dreams—a man profoundly dedicated to democracy. Terrorism thwarted Franco's plans for Carrero Blanco, who was assassinated by the Basque terrorist organization, "Euzkadi ta Azkatasuna" (or "ETA"), in 1973. The death of Carrero was a severe blow to Franco's plans for the position of Head of Government. Carrero had been one of Franco's most loyal and hard-line supporters, a man who would have stopped at very little to maintain authoritarianism in Spain. The doors for leadership succession in this particular position were thus left wide open.

International factors also played a role in bringing about change. The Spanish population and its leaders, especially in the business community, felt an increasing need and desire to become integrated into European economic structures. European Economic Community and North Atlantic Treaty Organization nations applied sometimes subtle and other times direct pressure on Spain to integrate into western economic and military structures. Extensive tourism and a large contingent of emigrant workers returning to Spain also had an internationalizing and liberalizing effect on the somewhat insular Spanish culture.

The realities of extensive social pluralization, a King dedicated to democracy and an awareness, even among authoritarian elites, that political change was necessary, culminated in a Spanish turning point toward democratization. Without long-term pluralization, there may not have been a compelling reason for the authoritarian elite to accept dramatic political change. If certain key "authoritarian" leaders had not favored democratization in and of itself, other, perhaps more violent, forms of political change could have followed Franco's death. The elite might have attempted a continuation of authoritarianism. Mounting social tensions would be met by severe repression which, in turn, could fuel a military coup, revolution or civil war. The results in Spain, however, were a peaceful transition to democracy, with a very elaborate, intense and prolonged constitution-making process.

Political Choices Before Democratization

The Choices in General

A single event is universally acknowledged as the watershed marking the end of Spain's authoritarian experience and the beginning of a new era—the death of Generalissimo Francisco Franco on November 20, 1975. Yet the transition only truly began when the political leaders answered the critical question of whether to pursue continuity, reform or "ruptura."

This question may arise at certain critical points during the existence of any authoritarian regime. The issue may come up at a time when the authoritarian elite is undergoing internal restructuring either due to the death of a preeminent figure or to a succession of leadership. It can also come up during national crises resulting from severe economic conditions, internal ethnic upheavals or adverse military conflicts. International pressures for change can become compelling during times of external military engagement. The viability of the authoritarian regime at such times may be severely threatened, especially if the external pressures are coupled with domestic dissatisfaction with the regime's policies. Examples of such externally aided turning points toward democratization were abundant at the end of World War Two in Germany, Austria, Italy and Japan. The Argentine junta's failure in the Falklands/ Malvinas War is a contemporary example of how external military defeat can aid in the breakdown of an authoritarian regime.

The choices made at any one of these critical periods in the life of an authoritarian regime often determine the nature of the political change, if any, that may follow. There may be continuity, with little or no change, if the leaders merely rearrange their roles within the authoritarian framework. A reformist turning point may take place if the authoritarian leaders engage in piecemeal policy changes promising an eventual democratization. If, however, there is abrupt political change, either at the instigation of the authoritarian elite or a powerful social group, a turning point of ruptura (break) may be in the making.

Intermediate choices are of course possible and indeed likely. The nature of the choice made may well help to determine the subsequent political climate. The elite's choice of continuity may mean repression and a potentially violent social reaction. A choice of reform may mean a slow and careful transition to democracy ripe with opportunities for authoritarian regression. Ruptura may mean a quicker, more chaotic and riskier transition to democracy.

Other consequences may lurk behind these choices as well. One of continuity in a country poised for transition will probably mean severe tension between the regime and society, possibly leading to harsh repression. Such a choice may also prompt revolutionary activity and preempt a peaceful transition to democracy. The consequences of Somoza's policies in Nicaragua may be so characterized.[4]

If a country is not ripe for transition, i.e., it neither displays much pluralization nor internal authoritarian elite dissent, the leaders' likely choice of continuity will proceed unobstructed, perhaps for years. Haiti at the time of Baby Doc Duvalier's succession of Papa Doc illustrates a successful case of continuity. Baby Doc Duvalier's choice of continuity was made infinitely easier by the fact that no developed social pluralization existed in Haiti at the time.[5]

If, on the other hand, the authoritarian elite choose to institute reformist measures aimed at eventual democratization, a slow reformist transition may take place. Facing growing social discontent and perhaps international pressures, the authoritarian elite choose controlled reform both to appease society and to liberalize the government slowly. However, the tentative quality of such reform may lead to a repeated postponement of actual regime change. Authoritarian Brazil during the 1970s illustrates such a case of slow reform with repeated postponements of actual regime change.[6]

Ruptura, finally, is a political choice that an authoritarian elite will seldom make. It may occur once a reformist transition is underway. Ruptura may come about as a choice made by pro-ruptura transitionary elites who, having been incorporated into the political process, gain the upper hand and stage a break with the authoritarian regime. Ruptura may also happen during an authoritarian regime breakdown. This type of ruptura is not preceded by a reformist transitionary phase but is instigated by an organized social segment which fills the vacuum of a disintegrating or unprepared authoritarian elite. The Portuguese transition to democracy began as a ruptura without a meaningful preceding reformist phase. A powerful social actor—the military—staged a bloodless coup to break with the disintegrating authoritarian regime. A similar choice of ruptura took place in the Philippines in 1986 when most of society, led by a charismatic leader aided by a powerful segment of the military, rose against the authoritarian leader, ousting him.[7]

Spain's Choice:
Continuity, Reform, Ruptura or Something Else?

At the time of Franco's death, there were several political factors favorable to the democratization of Spain. Among these were the assassination, two years earlier, of Premier Carrero Blanco. A substantial group of dissenting elites were developing, as well, within the authoritarian establishment. Internal social and external political pressures for reform and change were mounting. Moreover, unbeknownst to everyone at the time, the crowning of King Juan Carlos was critical in tipping the scale in favor of Spain's democratization.

The combination of these pressures and changes made the possible choice of continuity dangerous. To be sure, supporters of such a route existed. Among them were substantial sectors of Franco's military and police establishment. Pro-authoritarian feelings also existed in sections of the Catholic hierarchy, among far-right Falangists and other right-wing extremist groups, large landholding families and industrialists favored by Franco's economic policy. Paradoxically, terrorists and separatists of the extreme left, aiming at the violent destabilization of Spanish society, also favored a choice of continuity. Any other choice would deny these groups their raison d'etre.

Among those who favored reform were a wide variety of still illegal, mostly centrist, political parties and groups, sections of the Catholic Church and labor groups. Still others, including the "Partido Comunista Español" (Spanish Communist Party or "PCE"), the "Partido Socialista Obrero Español" (Spanish Socialist Workers' Party or "PSOE"), their trade unions, the CCOO and the UGT, respectively, and regional groups—especially in Catalonia and the Basque Country—favored a "ruptura democratica."

It is safe to say with hindsight that continuity would have been the most perilous and destabilizing choice in Spain. A choice of immediate ruptura could also have been politically suicidal for both the elite and society. Spain's collective political memory of the civil war was still strong enough to create the need for a moderate solution—a reformist one. What shape that reform would take and whether it would be accompanied by regime change rather than mere reform within the authoritarian system became a tantalizing question. The vast majority of the Spanish population favored some form of change, indeed expected change upon Franco's death. Finding out whether the majority of Spaniards desired democratization was not easy after forty years of censorship and repression. Choosing how to bring about any change became the formidable task of the King and of those who participated in post-Franco politics.

Arias Navarro's "Reform." In addition to the King, among those facing the political abyss were his newly appointed Prime Minister, Carlos Arias Navarro, and Torcuato Fernandez Miranda, the President of the influential Council of the Realm (a Francoist institution created to "direct" the King). This triumvirate and their appointees, including ministers, members of the Council of the Realm and Franco's appointed members of the Cortes, were to make the crucial decision of continuity, reform or ruptura. They did not have to look far for advice. The political opposition and a host of new characters and groups were quick to bring their views to the fore.

Arias Navarro's cabinet presented a mix of "Franquistas" and new faces, most of whom had been associated in one way or another with the authoritarian regime. The political, social and economic problems the government confronted were indeed many and ominous. Besides the overriding question of what path of reform to take, numerous immediate problems existed. Would individual and social rights remain curtailed or would some freedoms—of the press, of association—be allowed? Would Franco's political prisoners remain jailed or be given amnesty? Would the highly repressive law of August 7, 1975 on terrorism be further used, amended or repealed? How would immediate economic problems of inflation, unemployment and migrant workers returning en masse be handled?

In a January 28, 1976 speech, Arias announced a program of political reform. Most political groups, except the PCE, could hold private meetings upon 72-hour notice to the appropriate authorities. Street demonstrations would require governmental permission. The Arias program included small changes in the composition of Cortes. The executive would now control the appointment of only one-third (rather than a majority) of the upper house. The structure of the Council of the Realm was slightly revised but its critical role of selecting and nominating candidates for the position of prime minister remained intact. Arias did nothing to change the status of "Sindicatos," a monolithic institution designed by Franco to control labor activities. This and the other decisions were highly unpopular at a time of increasing labor difficulties and discontent. Described in detail before Cortes on April 28, 1976, Arias' reform package was a major disappointment to those favoring reform with regime change. His proposals were superficial and weak, described by many as "reform from above." His was a political program that did not increase popular participation in politics nor mitigate such harshly repessive laws as the aforementioned law on terrorism.[8]

The Suarez Reform Package. After only a few months of Arias Navarro's uninspired and half-hearted reform, King Juan Carlos dismissed his first prime minister. The new man on the job, Adolfo Suarez, was an unknown, young (43 years old) functionary from Franco's bureaucracy. Nobody would have guessed at the time that the King and Suarez would be the principal engineers of a political reform that would take Spain out of its authoritarian past and into a new constitutional order.

Adolfo Suarez presented an ultimately democratic package of political reform in September 1976. Cleverly disguised as a Fundamental Law, he called it the Eighth Fundamental Law and subtitled it "Ley para la Reforma Politica" (Law for Political Reform). The law, which was to become known by its subtitle, was not strictly Suarez' product. Instead, it was a product of broad political discourse between governmental and opposition politicians over a period of months. Among its more important provisions were changes in authoritarian institutions and statements of democratic principle. Among the latter were declarations affirming popular sovereignty, the supremacy of law, the inviolability of fundamental rights, universal suffrage and an implicit recognition of political pluralism. There was one significant omission, however—nowhere was there a repeal of Franco's Fundamental Laws.

Among Suarez' proposed institutional changes were democratizing changes in the composition of Cortes. It would become a bicameral body, consisting of a lower house or Congress of Deputies with 350 directly elected members, and an upper house or Senate with 207 members, some of whom would still be appointed by the King. The monarchy would retain most of the powers Franco had conferred upon it. The King would nominate the prime minister, appoint one-fifth of the Senate, submit any political question to a nationwide referendum, and dissolve Cortes and call for new elections at will. The Law for Political Reform implicitly allowed for the continued existence of Franco's Council of the Realm and Council of the Regency.[9]

This bridge-like law, which included both Francoist and democratic principles, was submitted to a popular referendum in December 1976. The results, as Table 2.1 shows, were overwhelmingly favorable to the new law. The significance of this double-edged law was that it allowed for a balanced transitionary period devoid of political extremism.

The Suarez government took subsequent democratizing steps during the first half of 1977. These included the elaboration of an electoral law, the scheduling of elections, the legalization of political parties, a broader amnesty for political prisoners and the preliminary recognition of some regional demands especially for the Basque Country and Catalonia. These events culminated in the holding of the first free elections in Spain in over forty years on June 15, 1977.

In 1976, the King, Suarez and members of the opposition had clearly achieved a new and original form of transition out of authoritarianism. They had engaged in a dynamic process of political dialogue and regime change. By cloaking democratic steps with authoritarian appearances, they diffused the potentially dangerous role of the political extremes. They used (and abused) Franco's framework of Fundamental Laws to break out of the authoritarian system "legally." Simultaneously, they utilized democratic devices (elections, freedom of the press) to usher in democracy. No other transition to democracy had ever started so auspiciously. Nowhere before had an elite camouflaged its democratizing intentions more cleverly. A ruptura with authoritarianism had taken place that avoided the dangers typical of dramatic political change. This process of combining the illusion of authoritarian legality with the reality of democratic practice without risking stability may best be described as "auto-ruptura."

Table 2.1 Results of the 1976 Referendum

Total Electoral Census	Number of Voters	Votes In Favor	Votes Against	Abstentions	Blank Ballots	Voided Ballots
22,644,290	17,599,662 (77.72% of Electorate)	16,573,180 (94.2% of those voting)	450,102 (2.6% of those voting)	22,270 (.12% of those voting)	523,457 (3% of those voting)	52,823 (.3% of those voting)

Source: Some information for this Table gathered from: Jorge de Esteban and Luis Lopez Guerra, De la Dictadura a la Democracia (Madrid: Servicio de Publicaciones, Facultad de Derecho), pp. 463-4.

The New Political Spectrum:
From One Party to "Hundreds"

There was a wide variety of illegal and alegal political groups in Spain at the time of Franco's death. The only legal party in the country was the forty-year-old "Movimiento Nacional" (National Movement), which by 1976 had little real or effective purpose. The history of the relationship between Generalissimo Franco and the "Movimiento Nacional" was one characterized often by moderate conflict and uncertainty. The authoritarian rather than totalitarian nature of Franco's rule had allowed for the semblance of limited pluralism in the elite conflict that often existed between "Movimiento" and government officials. During Franco's last years, however, the National Movement's ability to command respect and adherence, even from its own members (let alone the government), had dramatically declined.[10]

Shortly after Franco's death in November 1975, groups of all political persuasions came to the fore. By 1976 more than 200 would claim to be parties. Among them were associations historically recognized as parties—such as the PCE and the PSOE—and embryonic party forms that were to compete as "real" parties for the first time on June 15, 1977. Among these newly born parties were "Alianza Popular" (Popular Alliance or "AP") and "Union del Centro Democratico" (the Union of the Democratic Center or "UCD").

As Figure 2.1 illustrates, by early 1977, several parties and coalitions began to take shape. On the far right were minor Falangist and die-hard Francoist groups of tiny size and appeal and minimal potential as parties or even coalitional partners. However, also on the right was AP, a coalition of six rightist parties headed by Manuel Fraga Iribarne which was beginning to look like a major political force. During the precampaign and campaign periods, AP was considered a strong and potentially dangerous force because of its pro-Franco leanings.

Toward the center were a vast array of christian democratic, social democratic, regional, centrist, conservative and liberal groups, all claiming to be parties. These groups constantly entered into coalitions only to fall apart shortly thereafter. Some of these coalitions, such as the short-lived "Platajunta," included leftist groups. As the official campaign approached, many of these larger coalitions disintegrated into single parties or smaller coalitions. One of these smaller viable coalitions, of a center-right persuasion, was the UCD, an amalgam of moderate liberals and mild conservatives led by Suarez.

On the left was Suarez' toughest rival, a young, perhaps more charismatic politician, Felipe Gonzalez, leader of the historically (in the 1930s) popular PSOE. In 1977, however, the PSOE lacked an established

Figure 2.1 The Birth of the New Spanish Party System

Ideological Spectrum	Parties in 1976	Coalitions 1976 - 1977	Parties/Coalitions June 1977
Right	Democratic Reform Parliamentary Regional Group Union of Spanish People Spanish Democratic Union Spanish National Union Spanish National Front	AP	AP
Center Right	Popular Party Christian Democratic Left Social Democratic Federation Spanish Liberal Alliance	Democratic Center Independent Social Federation	UCD
Center	Spanish Democratic Union Popular Democrats	State Group	
Center Left	Christian Democrats Social Democrats Carlists PSOE Maoists		Christian Democrats Social Democrats Carlists PSOE PCE PSP Maoists
Left	PCE PSP Other left factions	Platform of Democratic Convergence "Junta Democratica" "Platajunta" [split]	
Regional Parties	Basque Parties & Groups Catalan Parties & Groups		PNV MC CC

Note: This figure incorporates only a fraction of the over 200 groups claiming to be political parties in 1976. The right-to-left spectrum is somewhat roughly drawn as some parties fluctuated in and out of coalitions that did not necessarily reflect their political philosophy. Although this figure does not follow the coalitional development of regional parties, many of these too worked in and out of coalitions throughout this period.

identity and popularity, especially among the largely youthful Spanish population. The party was also internally divided over whether it was primarily Marxist or social democratic. The PSOE's contemporary popularity stemmed namely from old republicans and new urban and blue collar workers. The fear of radicalism and of stirring up memories of the civil war partially explains why the PSOE was unable to command greater attention and respect during the pre-campaign and campaign.

Further to the left, emerging from the underground and exile, was the PCE. In the early 1960s, under the leadership of Santiago Carrillo, the party had sought democratic coalitions urging the non-violent transformation of Franco's regime. Following the Soviet invasion of Czechoslovakia in 1968 and intense internal party struggles, Carrillo and his "moderate" communism emerged victorious over the Stalinist wing of the PCE. This wing became a separate and "renovated" Spanish Communist Party strongly affiliated with and directed by the Soviets. Carrillo worked hard on legitimating the "democratic" image of the PCE by cultivating its "Eurocommunist" image and contacts, namely with the quintessential Eurocommunists, the Italian Communist Party. After much cloak and dagger intrigue, the PCE was finally legalized in April 1977, two months before Spain's first democratic elections in forty years.[11]

Farthest to the left were Marxist-Leninist, Trotskyite, Maoist and anarchist groups which, like the Falangists on the far right, were often opposed to the entire principle of democracy. To such parties, disinterested in participating, the elections were just another capitalist tool of exploitation.

There were still other significant parties or "quasi-parties." Among these were the regional parties of the Basque Country, principally the "Partido Nacional Vasco" (National Basque Party or "PNV"), and Catalonia, namely the "Convergencia Democratica Catalana" (Catalan Democratic Convergence "CC") and a more Marxist socialist party, the "Partido Socialista Popular" (Popular Socialist Party or "PSP"). Their size and local appeal made them parties of potential coalitional value to the larger ones—the UCD, PSOE, PCE and AP.

The elections of June 15, 1977 were preceded by a short three-week campaign. The UCD's appeal increased during these last weeks, partly due to the government's control of national television. Other parties had little time to organize coherent nationwide appeals and lacked the special media edge the government had. Abuses of the medium were not blatant, but non-UCD politicians were quick to complain about the "caretaker" government's technical advantage.

The election results, as Table 2.2 shows, confirmed these observations. To no one's great surprise, the UCD received the most votes (35 percent of the total popular vote) and seats in Cortes (165 out of a total of

Table 2.2   The Spanish National Election of 1977

Party or Coalition	Percentage of Votes	Number of Seats
UCD	35.0	165
PSOE	29.0	118
PCE	9.0	20
AP	8.0	16
CC	4.0	13
PNV	2.0	8
Other parties	13.0	10

Source: Information gleaned from various
periodical sources and the Central Electoral
Board as reported in El Pais and ABC, June –
July 1977.

350). Although not a majority, this result allowed Suarez to form a minority government through a coalition with other centrist and regional parties. Closely trailing the UCD with 29 percent of the popular vote and pleasantly surprising its followers, the PSOE received 118 seats in Cortes.

Both of the main parties on the political extremes made disappointing showings. AP, led by Fraga Iribarne, received 8 percent of the popular vote and 16 seats in Cortes while the PCE led by Santiago Carrillo received 9 percent of the vote and 20 seats. A relatively large residual percentage of votes—13 percent—went to several minor parties giving them a total of only 10 seats.

Although the results were not unexpected and no improprieties were evident, one of the major issues debated as a consequence of the elections was the fairness of the electoral system. As would be expected, the major defeated parties—namely the PSOE, PCE and AP—were the quickest to complain as they had the most to lose from the dubious proportionality of the new system (tailored around the d'Hondt system). Several technicalities worked in favor of the party with both the most votes and the most centrist or moderate position, i.e., the UCD. Among these favorable technicalities were the fact that each province (50) received four senators to represent it in the upper house regardless of proportionality. This allowed for equal representation of both rural and urban centers, the latter being more densely populated and liberal. Members of the lower house were chosen through proportional representation. Each province, however, no matter how small or sparsely populated, received a minimum of three representatives. Such representation clearly favored and over-represented several inland, rural and conservative Castilian provinces. Also favorable to the UCD was the fact that a large contingent of the (potentially leftist) voting population lived abroad—as migrant workers in northern Europe—and had questionable and difficult access to absentee ballots. In addition, a post-electoral subsidy system favored large parties capable of winning the election as only they would be able to repay their pre-election loans. Finally, the voting age was kept at 21 thus depriving a sizable, potentially more liberal-minded segment of society (18 to 21 year olds) from voting.[12]

In the translation of voting percentages into seating percentages, the big parties benefited directly from these arrangements. With exactly 34.7 percent of the vote, the UCD received 47.1 percent of the seats in Cortes. The PSOE, with 29.2 percent of the popular vote, received 33.7 percent of the seats. Meanwhile, the smaller parties suffered. The AP with 8.4 percent of the vote got only 4.6 percent of seats in Cortes, while the PCE, with 9.2 percent of the vote, received 5.7 percent of all seats (see Table 2.2).

Conclusion

By the end of June 1977 the stage was set for the further implementation of democracy in Spain. Parties were legal, elections had taken place, political amnesties had been given and other fundamental freedoms had begun to take root. Yet there still was no constitution, no basic document limiting the state and protecting the individual. During the summer of 1977 talks among representatives of the main political parties took place behind closed doors. One of the longest, most debated constitution-making processes of the post-World War Two period had started. It was not until December 1978, after several drafts and countless headaches, that Spain could officially call itself a constitutional democracy.

Notes

1. Juan J. Linz, "Opposition in and under an Authoritarian Regime: The Case of Spain," in Robert A. Dahl, ed., *Regimes and Oppositions* (New Haven, Conn.: Yale University Press, 1973), pp. 171–259.

2. Jose Amodia, *Franco's Political Legacy: From Dictatorship to Façade Democracy* (London: Allen Lane, 1977), pp. 92–96.

3. Amodia, pp. 36–39.

4. See generally, Thomas W. Walker, *Nicaragua: The Land of Sandino* (Boulder, Colo.: Westview Press, 1981), and, ed., *Nicaragua in Revolution* (New York, N.Y.: Praeger Publishers, 1981).

5. See generally, Edwin M. Martin, "Haiti: A Case Study in Futility," in *SAIS Review*, 2, Summer 1981, pp. 61–70.

6. See generally, Robert M. Levine, "Brazil: The Dimensions of Democratization," in *Current History*, 81, No. 472, Fall 1982, pp. 60–63 ff, and, William Overholt, ed., *The Future of Brazil* (Boulder, Colo.: Westview Press, 1978).

7. See generally, Kenneth Maxwell, "The Thorns of the Portuguese Revolution," in *Foreign Affairs*, 54, January 1976, pp. 250–70 and, L. S. Graham and H. M. Makler, eds., *Contemporary Portugal: The Revolution and its Antecedents* (Austin, Texas: University of Texas Press, 1979).

8. Other than periodicals, there is a paucity of literature tracing these developments. See generally, John F. Coverdale, *The Political Transformation of Spain After Franco* (New York, N.Y.: Praeger Publishers, 1979), and, Jorge de Esteban and Luis Lopez Guerra et al., *El regimen constitucional español* (Barcelona: Editorial Labor, S.A., 1980).

9. For more on this law, see the original law in "Ley 1/1977 de 4 Enero para la Reforma Politica," in *Boletin Oficial del Estado*, no. 4, 5 January 1977. For second-hand analyses, see: Pablo Lucas Verdu, *La Octava Ley Fundamental: Critica juridico-politica de la Reforma Suarez* (Madrid: Editorial Tecnos, 1976); Jose Maria Martin Oviedo, "De la Octava Ley Fundamental del Reino a la nueva ordenacion constitucional española," in *Revista de Derecho Publico*, nos. 68–69, July-December 1977; and, Luis Sanchez Agesta, "La nueva Ley fundamental para la Reforma Politica," in *Revista de Derecho Publico*, no. 66, January-March, 1977.

10. Juan J. Linz, "From Falange to Movimiento Organizacion: The Spanish Single Party and the Franco Regime," in Samuel Huntington and C. H. Moore, eds., *Authoritarian Politics in Modern Society* (New York, N.Y.: Basic Books, 1970), pp. 128–201.

11. There is a wide variety of literature on Eurocommunism. Among the more interesting is the PCE's own secretary general's piece: Santiago Carrillo, *Eurocommunism and the Spanish State* (Westport, Conn.: Lawrence Hill & Co., 1978).

12. Michael Roskin, "Spain Tries Democracy Again," in *Political Science Quarterly*, 93, Winter 1978–79, pp. 631–33.

Part 2

3

Technical Phases and Participants

The Stage Is Set

A handful of critical decisions must be made before a constitution-making process can begin. How do the transitionary elites decide what constitution-making route to take? What governmental entity is to initiate the first constitutional draft? Should such a body be elected or appointed? How are the drafters of the new fundamental text selected? What procedural steps or *technical phases* of approval should the draft go through, if any?

There are three major constitutional routes available to transitionary elites. The caretaker government, under the aegis of the executive branch, can appoint a commission of experts to draft the constitution. Once written, such a constitution can be submitted directly to a nationwide referendum. A more popular option involves calling for elections for the sole purpose of creating a constituent assembly. Such an assembly would have to dissolve itself prior to the implementation of the new constitution. Finally, the caretaker government may call for general elections (to be governed by temporary electoral laws) for a new general assembly which, once formed, would help in the drafting of the constitution. In contrast to the constituent variety, this type of assembly would continue to exist beyond the adoption of the new text. The peculiarity of this arrangement is clear—once the constitution is adopted, this pre-democratic assembly would continue to exist whether or not the new text sanctioned its institutional legitimacy.

Arguably, the most "democratic" mode of handling constitution-drafting is through the creation of a constituent assembly. In the Spanish case, however, much confusion and vagueness surrounded the subject. Nobody quite knew whether the June 15, 1977 elections would result in a "regularly" elected parliament (or Cortes) or an "extraordinarily" created constituent assembly. The political parties were divided on the issue. Liberal and leftist parties strongly favored the constituent option. The UCD, as the party in transitionary power, much preferred a regularly

35

elected parliament with its potentially longer lifespan. The UCD's views prevailed. Their victory would permit them to remain in power once the new constitution was adopted.

Beyond this strategic issue of choosing a constitution-making assembly are several tactical questions that need to be resolved early in the process. Would the constitutional draft be initiated by the government (or caretaker executive) and presented as a legislative proposal to Cortes? Or, would such a task be within the exclusive control of the Cortes without official executive participation?

After receiving some pressure on this matter from the PSOE and other parties, the government (and, obviously, the UCD) agreed not to interfere with the parliamentary nature of the process. While this promise was later broken, at the time it helped to keep the momentum of the transition going.

By late July 1977, it had become apparent that the parties with the greatest numerical and coalitional strength in Cortes would dictate the shape of the process. Such relative strength also directly translated into committee representation throughout the process.[1] Positioning themselves for this procedural competition, most parties were quick to announce their constitutional "platforms." Felipe Gonzalez of the PSOE stressed the "urgent need for a compacted constitution." The PCE's Secretary General, Santiago Carrillo, declared the need for a "government of national democratic concentration." Leopoldo Calvo Sotelo, representing the UCD, spoke of "three immediate objectives: a constitution, autonomies and economic measures." In the meantime, the AP, represented by Fraga Iribarne, had no qualms about declaring its loyalty "to the past." The regional representatives expressed their objectives a little more clearly. Jordi Pujol, a Catalan representative, said that "the concession of (regional) autonomies is of most special interest to the Crown." A Basque spokesman, Xabier Arzallus, warned that the "Basque Country must recover its political personality."[2]

After these initial declarations were made, the parties worked out a timetable and a set of rules for the elaboration of the new fundamental text. After some haggling and maneuvering, the parliamentarians finally agreed on seven technical phases for constitution-drafting (see Table 3.1).

The Technical Phases of Constitution-making

The Congressional Subcommittee Phase

The initial phase was in many ways the most important one. In it the framework of the new constitution was created and seven of the

Table 3.1   Technical Phases of Constitution-making in Spain, 1977 - 1978

Date	Technical Phase	Decision-making Body
22AUG77- 10APR78	I	<u>Congress of Deputies</u> Subcommittee on Constitutional Affairs
5MAY78- 20JUN78	II	Committee on Constitutional Affairs & Public Freedoms
4JUL78- 21JUL78	III	Plenary Session of the Congress
9AUG78- 14SEP78	IV	<u>Senate</u> Committee on the Constitution
25SEP78- 5OCT78	V	Plenary Session of the Senate
11OCT78- 25OCT78	VI	<u>Joint Committee of the Congress & the Senate</u>
31OCT78- 27DEC78	VII	Congressional Approval Senate Approval Popular Referendum Royal Sanction

most prominent political party representatives participated. The subcommittee was composed of three UCD politicians and one representative each from the PSOE, the PCE, the AP and a Catalan coalition, "Minoria Catalana" (Catalan Minority or "MC") (see Table 3.2).

The subcommittee began its official meetings on August 22, 1977. Leading up to this first meeting were intense internal party preparations for the talks. Throughout August the parties' constitutional proposals were released to the press and publically debated. Strict secrecy characterized the subcommittee's work from late August to November although some members made occasional but vague public statements.

Table 3.2   Members of the Congressional Subcommittee
            on Constitutional Affairs

Party Affiliation	Name of Representative
UCD	Gabriel Cisneros
	José Pedro Perez Llorca
	Miguel Herrero de Miñon
PSOE	Gregorio Peces Barba
PCE/PSUC	Jordi Solé Turá
AP	Manuel Fraga Iribarne
MC	Miguel Roca Junyent

Note: The Basques had no representative
       participating in these deliberations. The
       only regional presence was that provided by
       Roca Junyent of the MC.

At the end of November, however, major press leaks to *Cuadernos Para El Dialogo*, a political journal, and *El Pais*, a Madrid daily, took place.[3]

Lively public debates followed these leaks and continued until the end of the subcommittee's work. The subcommittee had completed three comprehensive reviews of the Preliminary Draft (or "Anteproyecto") and considered 1,333 amendments by the time it adjourned on April 10, 1978. On that date the seven members of the subcommittee signed the final Preliminary Draft of the Constitution.[4]

The Congressional Constitutional Committee Phase

The second technical phase ran from May 5, 1978 to June 20, 1978. Composed of thirty six members, the Congressional Committee on Constitutional Affairs and Public Liberties studied the Preliminary Draft, reviewed countless amendments and came up with its version of the new text—the Constitutional Project (or "Proyecto Constitucional").[5]

The Congressional Approval Phase

Once approved by the constitutional committee, the Constitutional Project was presented to the full house of the Congress of Deputies.

Following nearly another month of speeches, amendments and linguistic changes, the Congress voted overwhelmingly in favor of the Constitutional Project in late July 1978.[6]

The Senate Constitutional Committee Phase

Having overcome most of its congressional hurdles, the Constitutional Project began an obstacle course in the Senate. From late July to early August, many senators prepared proposed amendments. Even before this fourth technical phase began on August 18, 1,254 amendments had been formulated for presentation to the committee. As its first task, the committee tried to reduce the number of amendments by appealing to the parliamentary parties for restraint. Some parties, including the UCD, were inspired to reduce their proposed amendments. The committee's deliberations continued until September 14 when their review was completed.[7]

The Senate Approval Phase

The fifth technical phase lasted from September 25 through October 5, 1978 in the full house of the Senate. After overcoming initial difficulties and making further changes, the Senate finally approved a Senate version of the Constitutional Project.[8]

The Joint Constitutional Committee Phase

A sixth technical phase was necessary to reconcile the differing versions of the constitution approved by the Congress and the Senate. Composed of eleven members from both houses, the joint committee conducted secret and efficient talks. Their approved text became the Spanish Constitution of 1978.[9]

The National Approval Phase

The Constitution was overwhelmingly approved by both houses in separate votes on October 31, 1978 (see Tables 3.3 and 3.4). After an intense political campaign dominated by pro-constitutional forces but not entirely free of anti-constitutional and abstentionist overtones, the Spanish people enthusiastically approved the Constitution in a national referendum held on December 6, 1978 (see Table 3.5).[10] The final approval phase came to an end when the King ratified and sanctioned the new fundamental text on December 27, 1978 in a joint session of Cortes.

Beginning with the elections of June 15, 1977, and ending with the King's official signature, the Spanish constitution-making process lasted

Table 3.3   Final Votes on the Constitution in the Congress
            and the Senate

Decision-Making Body & Date	Total Members Present	Vote		
		Yes	No	Abstentions
Plenary Session of the Congress (Preliminary Vote 21 July 1978)	274	258	2	14
Plenary Session of the Senate*	--	--	--	--
Plenary Session of the Congress (Final Approval 31 October 1978)	345	325	6	14
Plenary Session of the Senate (Final Approval 31 October 1978)	239	226	5	8

Note: *There was no global preliminary vote on the
Constitution in the Senate; instead, each article was
voted on individually.

Source: Author's compilation from: Cortes: Diario de
Sesiones del Congreso de Diputados, No. 116, 21 July 1978,
p. 4591; Cortes: Diario de Sesiones del Senado, No. 67, 5
October 1978; Cortes: Diario de Sesiones del Congreso de
Diputados, No. 130, 31 October 1978, pp. 5182-85; Cortes:
Diario de Sesiones del Senado, No. 68, 31 October 1978,
pp. 3427-30.

over eighteen months and resulted in a text containing more than 160
articles. The Spanish constitutional experience had become one of the
lengthiest and most elaborate of the Twentieth Century.

The Protagonists

While an assessment of the political and coalitional strategies of the

Table 3.4   Negative Votes and Abstentions on the Constitution in the Congress and Senate

	Vote		
Decision-Making Body	Negative Vote Party/Member		Abstention Party/Member

Decision-Making Body	Negative Vote Party/Member		Abstention Party/Member	
Congress Plenary Session	AP:	Fernandez de la Mora Jarabo Paya Martinez Emperador Mendizabal Uriarto Silva Muñoz	AP:	Fuente de la Fuente Lapuerta y Quintero Pineiro Ceballos Elorriaga Zarandona
October 31, 1978	EE:	Letamendia Belzunce	PNV:	Cuerda Montoya Sodupe Curcuera Vizcaya Retana Aguirre Querexeta Arzalluz Antia Bujanda Sarasola
			UCD:	Aizpun Tuero
			MC:	Barrera Costa
			MG*:	Arana i Pelegri Morales Moya
	Total Number of Negative Votes: 6		Total Number of Abstentions: 14	
Senate Plenary Session	BG*:	Bajo Fanlo Bandres Molet	BG*:	Irujo Ollo Monreal y Zia Oregui Goenaga Zabala Alcibar
October 31, 1978	MG*:	Carazo Hernandez Xirinachs Damians	BG&R*:	Urfa Epelde
	MR*:	Gamboa	MR*:	Diez Alegria Salas Larrazabal
			MG*:	Audet Puncernau
	Total Number of Negative Votes: 5		Total Number of Abstentions: 8	

Note: * Meaning of abbreviations: BG: Basque Group; MG: Mixed Group; MR: Military Senator appointed by the King; BG&R: Basque Group Senator appointed by the King.

Source: Author's compilation from: Cortes: Diario de Sesiones del Congreso de Diputados, No. 130, 31 October 78, p. 5185; Cortes: Diario de Sesiones del Senado, No. 68, 31 October 78, p. 3430.

Table 3.5   Results of Spain's Constitutional Referendum
            of December 6, 1978

Total Electorate: 26,632,180

Total Votes Cast: 17,873,301 or 67.11%

Total Abstentions: 8,758,879 or 32.89%

Voted	Number of Votes	Percentage of Votes Cast	Percentage of the Electorate
YES	15,706,078	87.87	58.97
NO	1,400,505	7.83	5.25
BLANK	632,902	3.55	2.37
VOIDED	133,786	.75	.50

Source: El Pais, 22 December 1978, as reported by the
Central Electoral Board.

parties during the process is the single most important way to understand
the process, it is also useful briefly to mention the cast of characters
involved.[11] A complete compilation of biographical profiles of the literally
hundreds of participants in the process would be a herculean task. A
quick introduction to some of the principal protagonists is, however,
necessary.

Indirectly, the Spanish people decided on June 15, 1977, who among
the political parties would participate in the drafting of the constitution
(see Table 3.6). There was not, however, a direct translation of popular
vote into constitution-making clout. The largest parties definitely benefited, especially the UCD which with 35 percent of the total popular
vote received 47.14 percent or 165 congressional seats. The second largest
party, the PSOE, with 29 percent of the popular vote received 33.71
percent of the seats in Congress. As indicated in Chapter 2, the
parliamentary results strongly discriminated against the "major" minor
parties on the two political extremes—the PCE and the AP. Both parties
saw their popular vote percentages halved in the Cortes' seating dis-

tribution. While relatively limited in popular appeal, the regional parties received a percentage of seats roughly equivalent to their share of the popular vote (see Table 3.6). These initial distributions of power within Cortes would dictate the relative strength of the parties in the constitutional talks as well.[12]

Beyond the particular parties participating in the deliberations, were their shifting constitution-making coalitions. Among the most successful constitutional coalitions were the UCD/AP coalition centered around issues of "morality," and the UCD/PSOE/PCE/MC coalition which came to be known as the "consensus" coalition.

Among the most influential UCD members were its envoys to the congressional subcommittee, Jose Pedro Perez Llorca, Gabriel Cisneros and Miguel Herrero de Miñon. These individuals had a crucial hand in the creation of the constitutional framework and were actively involved in the process through its final stages, especially Perez Llorca who was also a member of the final joint committee.

Other UCD participants included the President of the Congress, Alvarez de Miranda, and the President of the Senate, Antonio Fontan. Each of them presided over the plenary sessions of their respective houses and participated directly in the joint committee. Some non-parliamentarian UCD participants also had roles in the shaping of the fundamental text. One of them was the Second Vice President of the Government, Fernando Abril, who played a crucial part in behind-the-scenes negotiations during the summer of 1978. He was directly involved in trying to keep the consensus coalition alive and in seeking constitutional support from the PNV which had strong reservations about the constitutional draft. Another more circumspect UCD participant was, of course, the President of the Government, Adolfo Suarez. Although never directly involved in the deliberations, Suarez held periodic meetings with his own and other party leaders, namely Felipe Gonzalez of the PSOE, Santiago Carrillo of the PCE and Manuel Fraga Iribarne of the AP.

The most visible socialist in the process was Gregorio Peces Barba. Both a member of the original subcommittee and the congressional committee, Peces Barba had a direct influence on the shaping of the draft and of the famous consensus coalition. He frequently hosted extra-parliamentary meetings among constitution-drafters either at his Madrid office or at his home in the outskirts. One of the more dramatic moments of the process took place when Peces Barba withdrew from the sub-committee on March 7, 1978 claiming that the UCD had reneged on a deal concerning the issue of regional autonomy.

Among other important PSOE participants were Enrique Mugica, Alfonso Guerra, a member of both the congressional committee and

Table 3.6   The Spanish Cortes of 1977

The Congress of Deputies (350 Members)

Party	Percentage of Total Popular Vote	Total Number of Seats	Percentage of Seats
UCD	35	165	47.14
PSOE	29	118	33.71
PCE	9	20	5.71
AP	8	16	4.57
CC	4	13	3.71
PNV	2	8	2.28
Other	13	10	2.86

The Senate (246 Members)

Party Affiliation	Total Number of Seats	Percentage of Seats
UCD Group	115	46.37
Socialist Group	48	19.75
Independent Socialists & Progressives	23	8.87
Entesa dels Catalans	15	6.04
Independent Grouping	13	5.24
Mixed Group	13	5.24
Independent Group	10	4.03
Basque Group	9	3.62

Sources: Information gathered from: Cortes: Diario de Sesiones del Congreso de Diputados, Cortes: Diario de Sesiones del Senado, El Pais and ABC, June - September 1977.

the joint committee and, of course, Felipe Gonzalez, who as party leader played both an extra-parliamentary role similar to that of Suarez and a direct role as a voting member of the congressional committee. Another notable socialist was Enrique Tierno Galvan, a renowned scholar, who had led the other socialist party, the PSP, from the inception of the transition. Upset about his exclusion from the subcommittee, Tierno did, however, become a voting representative to the congressional committee and later joined forces with the PSOE in a PSOE/PSP merger.

Among other parties' outstanding participants were Fraga Iribarne and Silva Muñoz of the AP, Jordi Sole Tura, representing a communist coalition, and Santiago Carrillo, Secretary General of the PCE. Fraga was one of the most active and flamboyant characters of the process, never afraid to defend the past. His fellow AP member, Silva Muñoz was even less quiet about his right-wing preferences. Also prominent were several regional leaders—Roca Junyent, Barrera Costa, Reventos and Jordi Pujol among the Catalans and Arzallus, Letamendia and Garaicoechea, leader of the PNV, among the Basques.

A few crucial indirect participants also had an impact on the process. Among the most notable of these was the King who, throughout the process, maintained a neutral but reassuring presence. He often hosted talks among the various party and government leaders and, in speeches, reaffirmed his democratic beliefs. Other indirect "influentials" included representatives from two pillars of Franco's authoritarianism—the Catholic Church and the military establishment. Each institution, through its spokesmen (usually an archbishop or a general), made visible efforts to adapt to democratizing realities. The military often voiced its desire to become "apolitical" while remaining the defender of law and order. The Church, afraid of losing its previously privileged position vis-a-vis the state, worried publicly about potential changes in the "moral fiber" of Spain.

The academic community provided another special group of participants. They were sometimes involved directly, as was Oscar Alzaga, a UCD representative to the congressional committee, and other times indirectly, as was Pablo Lucas Verdu, a prominent constitutional scholar. This well-informed group led an intense, and often highly critical debate over parts of the various constitutional drafts. Their debate and critique had a measurable impact on the final form and substance of the constitution. Their contribution proved not only legally substantive but at times even grammatical.

A final assortment of groups could not be ignored—those who neither participated directly nor indirectly in the process but were active bystanders. These groups were either refused access to the process for lack of popular electoral support or consciously decided not to participate because of their political beliefs. Among these were extra-parliamentary groups on the political extremes such as the "Liga Comunista Revolucionaria" (Revolutionary Communist League or "LCR") and "Fuerza Nueva" (New Force or "FN"), led by Blas Piñar, a neo-fascist. Terrorist groups, such as ETA, were also part of this group of active non-participants as they conducted violent acts in an attempt to interfere with the successful denouement of the process and the overall transition. Once the national approval phase began in late 1978, many of these groups encouraged abstentionism or a rejection of the constitution during the popular referendum.

This was the panorama of direct and indirect participants, observers, critics and outsiders who in one way or another had or tried to have an impact on the Spanish constitution-making process. The analysis of the coalitional strategies and phases of the process that follows reveals how and why it developed as it did to a successful conclusion.

Notes

1. See Table 4.1 in Chapter 4.
2. See *El Pais* and *ABC*, 28 July 1977. Author's translation.
3. See *El Pais*, 23–25 November 1977.
4. See *El Pais* and *ABC*, 11 April 1978.
5. See *El Pais* and *ABC*, from 5 May 1978 through 22 June 1978. Also see, *Cortes: Diario de Sesiones del Congreso de Diputados*, Nos. 59–93, 5 May 1978 through 20 June 1978.
6. See *El Pais* and *ABC*, from 4 July 1978 through 22 July 1978. Also see, *Cortes: Diario de Sesiones del Congreso de Diputados*, Nos. 103–116, 4 July 1978 through 21 July 1978.
7. See *El Pais* and *ABC*, from 1 August 1978 through 12 August 1978 and 15 September 1978. Also see, *Cortes: Diario de Sesiones del Senado*, Nos., 39–55, 18 August 1978 through 14 September 1978.
8. See *El Pais* and *ABC*, 6 October 1978. Also see, *Cortes: Diario de Sesiones del Senado*, Nos. 58–67, 25 September 1978 through 5 October 1978.
9. See *El Pais* and *ABC*, 12–13 October 1978, 18–20 October 1978 and 26 October 1978.
10. See *El Pais* and *ABC*, 1 November 1978. Also see, *Cortes: Diario de Sesiones del Congreso de Diputados*, No. 130, 31 October 1978 and, *Cortes: Diario de Sesiones del Senado*, No. 68, 31 October 1978.
11. See Chapter 4 for an analysis of the coalitional strategies of the Spanish political parties during the constitution-making process.
12. See Chapter 4 for an elaboration on this observation.

4

Coalitional Strategies and
Political Phases

A useful analysis of a constitution-making process begins with an inquiry into the practical relevance of each participating political party. The relative clout of each party stems from both its numerical and its qualitative presence throughout the technical phases of the process. The qualitative strength of each party has, in turn, a direct impact on its coalitional behavior. Tracing the parties' coalitional behavior through the technical phases of the process yields a set of political phases. This coalitional/political phase analysis is the single most useful way to understand the development and outcome of the constitution-making process.

Party Relevance

The Parties' Numerical Presence in the Process

The numerical strength of each party in Cortes was already summarized in Chapter 3. Simply put, the UCD far outnumbered other parties in both its share of parliamentary seats and presence in each of the technical phases of constitution-drafting. The UCD's average overall numerical presence in the process was 44.86 percent (see Table 4.1).

Almost equally important, in terms of its 29 percent share of the popular vote, was the PSOE. Its presence through the technical phases of the process did not translate as favorably as did that of the UCD. Ranging from a low presence of 14.28 percent in the subcommittee to a high of 36.11 percent in the congressional committee, the PSOE's average overall presence in the process was 24.41 percent (see Table 4.1).

Table 4.1 Constitutional Subcommittee and Committees by Party Affiliation

Number of Representatives & Percentage of Total Representation in Each Committee

Political Party or Coalition	Congressional Subcommittee (Aug77-Apr78) 7 Members	Congressional Committee (5May78-20Jun78) 36 Members	Senate Committee (9Aug78-14Sep78) 25 Members	Joint Committee (11Oct78-25Oct78) 11 Members
UCD	3 (42.85%)	17 (47.2%)	11 (44%)	5 (45.45%)
PSOE	1 (14.28%)	13 (36.11%)	5 (20%)	3 (27.27%)
PCE/PSUC	1 (14.28%)	2 (5.55%)	0	1 (9.09%)
AP	1 (14.28%)	2 (5.55%)	0	0
PNV	0	1 (2.77%)	1 (4%)	0
MC	1 (14.28%)	1 (2.77%)	2 (8%)	1 (9.09%)
Mixed Group	0	0	2 (8%)	0
Independents	0	0	4 (16%)	1 (9.09%)

Source: Author's compilation from: El Pais, May - October 1977. Statistical percentages are the author's elaboration.

The next numerically significant parties were the coalitionally important PCE and AP. The PCE had envoys to three of the four major committees, while the AP was only present in the initial subcommittee and congressional committee. Its average overall presence reached only 4.95 percent while its share of the popular vote had been 8 percent (see Table 4.1). The PCE, with only a slightly higher share of the popular vote (9 percent), averaged a 7.23 percent presence in three of the technical phases of the process (see Table 4.1).

The final two influential groups in the process were the regional parties. The Catalans by far outnumbered the Basques in directly participating in the process. They had representatives in four of the more influential decision-making bodies (see below) averaging a presence of 8.53 percent which was significantly higher than their 4 percent share of the popular vote (see Table 4.1). Although the Basques theoretically benefited from the Catalans' pro-regional outlook, their presence was limited and intermittent. They only had one representative each to the congressional and senate committees. Their average presence in the process of 1.69 percent did, however, correspond fairly closely to their 2 percent share of the popular vote (see Table 4.1). Together, of course, the regional parties had a substantial presence throughout the process (10.22 percent) making their demands difficult to ignore and giving them potential bargaining power as coalitional partners.

The Relative Significance of Each Committee

In order to assess the relative weight of each party in the process, it is also necessary to rank the various technical phases. Of the four major decision-making bodies—the subcommittee, congressional committee, senate committee and joint committee—the initial subcommittee was the most decisive. In it the overall framework of the constitution was delineated, and an agenda of urgent political issues was set. Major decisions were made guaranteeing fundamental democratic rights, creating a formula for regional autonomy, designating the regime a parliamentary monarchy, separating subtly the church from the state and endorsing a free market economy. The fact that seven prominent Spanish politicians worked closely together in this subcommittee added to the relevance and influence of its eventual product, the Preliminary Draft. Each of these men exerted a direct influence on the balance of the constitutional deliberations as well. The approved Spanish Constitution of 1978 remained relatively unchanged from the subcommittee's Preliminary Draft.[1]

The second most important committee was the Congressional Committee on Constitutional Affairs and Public Freedoms. In it, the political mechanics outlined in the subcommittee's Preliminary Draft were refined and hammered out. Amendments were presented, attacked, defended and sometimes adopted. Among the committee's members were some of the most influential and visible figures in Spanish politics including Felipe Gonzalez, leader of the PSOE, Santiago Carrillo, Secretary General of the PCE, Manuel Fraga Iribarne, leader of the AP, and the remaining subcommittee members. While the subsequent senate committee rejected some of the congressional committee's solutions, in cases of direct conflict between the congressional and the senate drafts, the final joint committee more frequently opted for the congressional version.

This last point leads to the joint committee's ranking as the third most significant committee in the process. Supposedly neutral in character and function, this committee not only smoothed out minor linguistic differences between the congressional and senate texts but, in cases of substantive conflict, had the power of deciding which text would prevail. The political parties were well aware of the significance of this committee and wasted no time in trying to place their respective representatives in it. Intense political jockeying ensued to decide who would integrate the joint committee. In the end, a three-way agreement between the UCD, the PSOE and the MC to man this committee saved the day.[2]

While ranking fourth in relative importance to the process, the senate committee should not be underestimated. In it significant battles were fought and political cliff-hangers developed especially concerning regional issues. It is however ranked fourth because most of the changes it made were either cosmetic or did not withstand the scrutiny of the joint committee.

The third and fifth technical phases of the process—the plenary sessions in the Congress and Senate—rank last in qualitative importance. Although often exciting, these phases mainly served as approvals of the work done by the respective preceding committees.

Coalitional Strategies

The party with the greatest coalitional capabilities was, of course, the UCD with a total of thirty-six representatives present in the four most important phases. Its constant numerical advantage gave it an impressive coalition-making advantage. An association with any one of the other parties—excluding the Basques—could provide it with a winning coalition. From the inception to the adoption of the new constitution, the UCD thus had a pervasive influence on the process and outcome.

The PSOE was the next coalitionally important party with a total of twenty-two representatives in the four critical committees. In order to succeed, however, unless it coalesced with the UCD, the PSOE would always have to seek coalitions with two or more other parties. More often than not, such coalitional needs created obstacles for the achievement of PSOE goals.

Surprisingly, the next coalitionally significant group was not the PCE or the AP, but the MC. Unlike the former two, the MC had representatives in each of the four important committees, giving them the opportunity to influence the process in each of its critical phases. In order to gain its regional goals, the MC needed to forge coalitions with either the PSOE and several other parties or the UCD.

Both the AP and PCE rank next in coalitional significance. While the PCE had greater numerical representation in the process with a total of four representatives in three committees (as contrasted to the AP's total of three representatives in the first two technical phases), the AP had a weighty coalitional advantage. Because of its conservative outlook, the AP had the ability of forming a winning coalition with the UCD. Such a UCD/AP coalition actually formed in the two most qualitatively important committees—the subcommittee and congressional committee (see Table 4.2). Such an association had the potential of becoming a dominant coalition throughout the process. Aware of the dangers of such a winning right-wing coalition, UCD leaders had sufficient foresight to only intermittently and selectively coalesce with the AP.

The PCE maintained a moderate tone throughout the talks. It almost always followed the lead of the PSOE and the MC forming part of both the PSOE/PCE/MC/PNV coalition and the "consensus" coalition that included the UCD (see Table 4.2). The PCE's low profile made it a coalitional partner of only secondary significance. The only party to whom the PCE could have been useful for a majority coalition would have been the UCD. An exclusive UCD/PCE coalition was, however, unlikely given the alternative parties available to the UCD for a winning coalition (see Table 4.2).

Ranking last in coalitional importance was the PNV. With a total of two representatives to the congressional and senate committees, the PNV was frequently alone in its regional demands, which often went beyond those of the MC. The PNV's influence on the process derived mostly from its extra-parliamentary activities—in its behind-the-scenes negotiations with the government and the consensus coalition, in its ability to mobilize popular demonstrations in the Basque Country and in its frequent and emotional public statements and press releases. The PNV's intense negotiations with the consensus coalition proved fruitless in its judgment. Ultimately, however, the party did have an impact on the regional provisions of the new Spanish Constitution. While such influence did not translate into a progressive regional formula, it had

Table 4.2   Coalitional Strategies in Cortes during the
            Constitution-making Process

Political Phase	Dominant Coalition(s)	Other Unsuccessful Coalition(s)	Non-Coalesced Parties
Consensual Agenda Setting Phase & Publicizing & Mobilizing Phase	1. The Consensual Coalition 2. UCD/AP	PSOE/MC/ PCE	PNV
Dissensual Pre-Congressional Phase	1. UCD/AP 2. UCD/MC/PCE		PNV PSOE
Consensual Parliamentary Phase	1. The Consensual Coalition 2. UCD/AP	PSOE/MC/ PCE (+PNV)	PNV AP
Constrained Parliamentary Phase	1. The Consensual Coalition 2. PSOE/PCE/ MC/PNV/ & 3 Senators Appointed by the King	PSOE/MC/ PCE (+PNV)	PNV AP

Note: The parties listed under the "non-coalesced" column are
only those relevant parties in the Cortes that actually, at one
time or another, coalesced with other parties.

a definite moderating effect on the potentially successful conservative
trends present in the constitution-making process.

The Meaning of *Consenso*

The word *consenso* was often used in the Spanish transitional context.
It was a term frequently associated with the political maneuverings of
the constitution-makers. Hardly a day passed in which the Madrid press
did not refer to the survival or demise of consensus politics. On another
level, *consenso* also became the object of political analysis and observation. *Consenso* was indeed a novel form of political negotiation in
Spain, conducive to broadly based coalitions and solutions. It involved

the use of whatever means necessary—secret and public, parliamentary and extra-parliamentary—to achieve political compromise. The downside of this practice was that overly negotiated solutions were often vague or ambiguous. While *consenso* provided an effective focus for negotiation by bringing divergent political forces together, the results were often less than crisp and useful.

In practical terms, the significance of *consenso* to the Spanish transition cannot be underestimated. *Consenso* was not merely a mode of negotiation, it referred to a specific coalition during the constitution-making process. The "consensus coalition" became the most successful political force of that period. The parties constituting this group—the UCD, PSOE, PCE and MC—were more than heterogeneous. The consensus coalition was one integrated by forces of the left, the center-right and the regions. Given the sociopolitical and regional makeup of Spain, no other coalitional force could have carried as much legitimacy as this one. Each of the coalitional actors contributed necessary ingredients for a workable constitutional solution.

The Political Phases of Constitution-making

Unlike the bureaucratically discernable technical phases, the political phases of constitution-making are a more subtle set of constitutional steps. Each political phase captures a distinct coalitional development. An analysis that traces the coalitional behavior of the constitution-makers therefore yields a set of political phases. These in turn provide a crucial tool with which to understand the nature of the entire process. Unlike the purely descriptive technical phases, the political phase analysis yields insights into how and why a constitution-making process succeeds or breaks down.

There are several ingredients that go into the analytical breakdown of the Spanish process into six political phases. First is the degree of openness (publicity) or secrecy of the constitutional deliberations. Related to this factor is the parliamentary or extra-parliamentary nature of a particular set of talks. Whether the negotiations are mostly accommodational or confrontational in nature is a second major factor. Also important is whether the talks are protracted or swift, especially where thornier issues are under consideration. The breadth of a particular "winning" coalition at a given time is a final critical factor. When several of these conditions discernably change, it is likely that a new political phase is emerging. For instance, when negotiations that have been largely accommodational terminate, drifting into a distinctly confrontational mood (that is clearly not momentary), a new phase is developing. With this in mind, let us turn to the political phases of constitution-making in Spain (see Table 4.3).

The Consensual Agenda-setting Phase

This phase spans the first half of the subcommittee's work from August to mid-November 1977. The subcommittee members carried out these deliberations largely in secret, within parliamentary boundaries and in a cooperative yet somewhat painstaking manner. Their principal task was to identify and prioritize the most crucial issues to be addressed, and hopefully resolved, through the Constitution.

Among the most important issues the subcommittee tried to resolve was that of characterizing the new political system. Their first draft would contain the ultimate solution—Spain would be a parliamentary monarchy. A second critical issue involved the territorial reorganization of Spain. Would it be a federation of regions or would some variation on Franco's unitary state be developed? The basic contours of the subcommitee's ambiguous territorial proposal—mixing ingredients from both the unitary and federal formulas—survived largely unchanged into the final version of the Constitution. Guaranteeing and defending fundamental democratic freedoms was another crucial task the subcommittee firmly addressed. The apoliticization or elimination of Francoist social and political institutions, namely "Sindicatos," the Council of the Realm, the Catholic Church and the military establishment was yet another formidable constitutional task the subcommittee handled. The constitution-makers also drafted provisions concerning the domestic and international economic organization of Spain. Many of the subcommittee's major points, as memorialized in their Preliminary Draft, were to survive basically unchanged throughout the process. The overall framework of the Spanish Constitution of 1978 was fundamentally hammered out in the subcommittee.

When the Preliminary Draft was leaked to the press in early November, the generally secretive and consensual nature of the process changed overnight. Blamed on the PSOE, which vehemently denied it, this leak opened up a Pandora's Box of constitutional deliberations. Those who until then had been excluded or quiet suddenly spoke out against both the secretive and the consensual nature of the process.

This first political phase of the Spanish constitution-making process was thus one characterized by largely secret, parliamentary and accommodational behavior, dominated by a broadly based coalition—the consensus coalition—and yielding what seemed to be broadly compromised solutions.[3]

Table 4.3 The Political Phases of Constitution-making in Spain

Duration	Political Phase	Characteristics		
		Dominant Coalition	Negotiations	
August 1977 to mid-November 1977	Consensual Agenda Setting Phase	The Consensual Coalition	Accommodation Multilateralism	
November 1977 to beginning March 1978	Publicizing & Mobilizing Phase	The Consensual Coalition	Accommodation Multilateralism	
March 1978 to beginning May 1978	Dissensual Pre-Congressional Phase	UCD/AP Coalition	Confrontation Unilateralism	
May 1978 to end July 1978	Consensual Parliamentary Phase	The Consensual Coalition	Accommodation Multilateralism	
July 1978 to beginning October 1978	Constrained Parliamentary Phase	The Consensual Coalition	Accommodation Confrontation Multilateralism	
October 1978 to end December 1978	Consensual Approval Phase	The Consensual Coalition	Accommodation Multilateralism	

The Publicizing and Mobilizing Phase

The publication of the Preliminary Draft in *Cuadernos Para El Dialogo* and *El Pais* set off a political chain reaction. An array of rash accusations between the constitution-makers quickly changed the until then cordial nature of the talks. Secrecy gave way to a broad public debate in which political parties and others actively sought to publicize their views and mobilize support. Even such low-profile actors as the Catholic Church and the military became instant critics of the draft.[4]

During the last months of 1977 other disturbing extra-constitutional incidents contributed to the heightened tension. Large scale rioting and vandalism, stemming from regional celebrations, erupted in Malaga (Andalusia) and the Canary Islands. Jail rioting spread throughout the country shortly thereafter. These incidents contributed to the constitutional debate on law and order, which was epitomized by a virulent exchange between Santiago Carrillo and Manuel Fraga Iribarne in Cortes. Four days later there was renewed political violence in the Basque Country.[5]

On January 5, 1978, the Cortes officially published the Preliminary Draft. Each party was quick to publicize its disagreements with the text. AP had great difficulties with the use of the word "nationalities" to describe Spain's regions. The PSOE expressed reservations with the creation of a "Parliamentary Monarchy" rather than a republic. The UCD, as the governmental party, voiced objections to the inclusion of a non-constructive vote of no confidence in parliamentary procedure. The regional parties were deeply dissatisfied with what seemed to be emerging as the territorial formula for Spain.[6]

Over the ensuing two months, 1,133 amendments were presented to the subcommittee. During this largely quiet period, *El Pais* began reporting that the preceding consensual mood seemed to be returning to the subcommittee talks as they studied the proposed amendments.[7] In early March, a dramatic twist of events shattered these expectations.

The second phase, unlike the first, was thus replete with public and extra-parliamentary activities. While it could not be fully characterized as a dissensual period as the constitution-makers still practiced accommodational behavior, the phase definitely contained the seeds of dissension.

The Dissensual Pre-Congressional Phase

On March 7, 1978 what had seemed to be a trend toward consensus suddenly changed. Gregorio Peces Barba, the PSOE's subcommittee representative, withdrew from the proceedings after accusing the UCD of breaking a painstakingly negotiated set of compromises. Simultaneously, a large section of Prime Minister Suarez's cabinet resigned and a new, considerably more conservative group of ministers was appointed. The press construed these changes as a "turn to the right."[8]

A few days after Peces Barbas' withdrawal from the talks, Suarez and Felipe Gonzalez held a summit. The socialist leader outlined his party's conditions for returning to the deliberations. The PSOE had major problems with the UCD's support of articles 16, 28, 32 and 33, which dealt with religious, educational and economic issues. The UCD, contrary to compromises made, now proclaimed its support of the Catholic Church's continued official involvement in education and with-drew its support of some state involvement in the economy.[9]

Agreement among the remaining subcommittee members also seemed to have broken down. Although the PCE bitterly condemned the PSOE for abandoning the talks, what was left of these deliberations was also conflictual. As one representative, Miguel Roca, reported "the only consensus that exists is that we must finish the work."[10] The largest thorn in everyone's side was the regional issue. Even in the absence of the socialist delegate, the subcommittee continued to hammer out another revised draft. Against the continuous objections of AP, a very tenuous coalition among the UCD, PCE and MC pushed through the final revisions to the draft.

On April 5, 1978, the revised Preliminary Draft was ready for submission to the congressional committee. Under protest, Peces Barba nevertheless signed this draft together with the other six subcommittee members on April 10, 1978. While projecting an uneventful outward appearance, the parties of the consensus coalition, including the PSOE, began holding secret talks to resuscitate their coalition for the next round of congressional deliberations.

The third political phase of the Spanish constitution-making process was the first purely dissensual one. In it a principal player—the PSOE—removed itself from the consensual coalition and publically opposed a member of that coalition—the UCD. In it as well, the spectre of a right-wing UCD/AP coalition that could survive unscathed throughout the talks also appeared. Such a coalition could single-handedly force the approval of a right-wing constitution.

The Consensual Parliamentary Phase

The congressional committee opened its talks on May 5, 1978. Composed of thirty-six members and presided over by Emilio Attard, the debates had an auspicious beginning. Almost every participant encouraged a return to consensual negotiations. On May 6, 1978 the political forces forming the consensual coalition seemed to have reached a new plateau of accommodation. Almost simultaneously, Felipe Gonzalez began to characterize the PSOE as a social-democratic rather than a Marxist socialist party.[11]

The committee approved several articles over the next few weeks at a moderately brisk pace. At first, there were indications that a UCD/AP coalition would emerge around several major issues. Among these were the inclusion of the words "order" and "social peace" in the regulation of individual freedoms and opposition to extending the civil rights of eighteen-year-olds beyond voting. The UCD/AP coalition favored a continued relationship between the Catholic Church and the state and opposed the abolition of the death penalty. Needless to say these positions were diametrically opposed to those of the PSOE/PCE/MC coalition.

Several times the UCD threatened the stability of the consensual coalition by trying to introduce spot amendments on already negotiated issues. Among these were the UCD's attempts at limiting the rights of the detained and increasing the state's ability to prevent terrorism. Faced with the prospect of a consensual coalition breakdown, the UCD summarily withdrew some of these surprise proposals. A UCD spokesman, Rafael Arias Salgado, quickly reassured politicians and the public alike that the UCD would "do nothing to endanger the constitutional consensus."[12] The consensual tone of the talks was confirmed shortly thereafter as a more systematic PSOE/UCD understanding seemed to emerge. A major consensual breakthrough took place after PSOE representative Alfonso Guerra and UCD/governmental envoy Fernando Abril, among others, held secret nocturnal meetings achieving a broad agreement on the until then thorny issue of education.[13]

Concomitant with the rapprochement between the UCD and the PSOE was the increasing marginalization (and self-marginalization) of certain minorities, namely the AP and the Basques. The other two constitution-makers—the PCE and the MC—followed the coalitional lead of the PSOE. With some notable exceptions, the tenuous consensual (UCD/PSOE/PCE/MC) coalition would dominate the balance of the constitution-making process even though its negotiations were always intense and often verged on breakdown. Meanwhile, the AP's inflexible conservatism and the Basques' extreme regionalism had the effect of increasingly distancing them from the process. Their self-marginalization would also eventually antagonize the consensual partners some of which represented positions sympathetic to those of the AP or PNV.

Through the remainder of May, the consensual formula continued to work. In a single day twenty-six constitutional articles containing previously sticky issues were approved. Tension, however, was never far beneath the surface. Heated debates took place on the role of the

Monarch and what type of electoral system to constitutionalize. Forces of the left and center-left strongly backed a system of proportional representation while the UCD, joined by the AP, favored a majority system. A last-minute compromise, however, saved the consensual agreement on these issues. Accommodation had again been achieved through extra-parliamentary means in meetings attended by the consensual partners and, according to the press, even Prime Minister Suarez.[14]

Optimistic reports about an overall constitutional agreement appeared during this period. The press discovered and reported extra-parliamentary nocturnal meetings at Peces Barba's office. While such escapades were frequent, the novelty of the June 1978 meetings was that they were regularly attended by Fernando Abril, the Second Vice President of the UCD Government. At the center of these night-time meetings was a consensual effort to resolve the regional problem.

Throughout this period, the AP intensified its attack on the consensual nature of the process. It reacted sharply against the aforementioned extra-parliamentary meetings. As Silva Muñoz declared to *Hojas del Lunes*, the secret meetings were "inadmissible, anti-parliamentary and anti-democratic."[15]

After 148 hours of congressional debate and 1,342 speeches, the congressional committee finalized its work on June 20, 1978 at 9:45 PM. The accommodational nature of the deliberations was confirmed as the major parties hailed their constitutional draft as a consensual fundamental text. Remembering the words of Azaña during the constitutional process of 1931, Emilio Attard, the president of the committee, declared that "the constitution is a piece of clothing that must fit us all."[16]

The plenary sessions of the Congress confirmed the basic agreements achieved in the committee. As in the committee, tension and excitement over some of the more divisive issues was always present. The Basques and the AP were the loudest as they gained the chance, in the full chamber, to vent their objections to the work of the consensual coalition. The Basques were sometimes more successful than the AP. In one instance, a suggested PNV amendment effectively countered a UCD proposal limiting the rights of the detained during a state of exception. Widely hailed as a progressive victory, this PNV amendment was roundly supported by leftist, centrist and social democratic forces.[17]

Otherwise, the PNV did not see much in the way of success. Throughout July, extra-parliamentary talks between the government and the Basques intensified, with the former trying to bring the latter into the mainstream. The greatest sticking point concerned the Basques' demand for the restoration of historical foral rights which they had enjoyed during the Second Republic and Franco had cancelled. During the final plenary sessions of Congress, sharp attacks and confrontations between the Basques and conservatives ensued. In the final days of congressional debate, violence intensified in the Basque Country, culminating, on the date the Preliminary Draft was overwhelmingly approved by the Congress, in the assassination of two military men (see Table 3.3). All parties equally condemned the incident. Felipe Gonzalez commented that "nothing happens by chance or by accident. The day was chosen."[18] During these final days of congressional negotiation the largely consensual and cooperative atmosphere gave way to a period of greater tension and renewed violence.

The consensual phase was thus one in which the majority coalition comprised of both the UCD and the PSOE, among others, succeeded in agreeing and compromising on some of the toughest issues of the day. The phase was also characterized by the increased marginalization of the more extreme parties—namely the AP and the PNV Basques. While attempts at bringing these parties into the mainstream generally failed, the period was nevertheless successful in that the parties of the center and the moderate left and right maintained a coherent approach to constitution-making. Events outside of the process per se—such as violence in the regions—bore the greatest responsibility for changing the political mood of the talks.

The Constrained Parliamentary Phase

The key ingredients in this changed atmosphere were the Basque problem and a reawakening of PSOE/UCD tensions within the Senate. While the consensual coalition never quite broke down during this period, its endurance was certainly tested. At the end of this phase, the consensual coalition was in fact at its strongest.

The first tensions between the UCD and the PSOE became apparent on August 11, when the former presented amendments to articles which it had heavily negotiated with the PSOE. To the great chagrin of the socialists, the UCD achieved a modification of article 25 concerning education.[19] The UCD continued to introduce amendments and on September 13 threatened the stability of the consensual coalition by introducing broad new proposals limiting regional autonomy. These suggestions instantly antagonized both the left and regional forces who banded together in a bitter confrontation against the UCD, accusing it of bad faith and irresponsibility. The following day, with the unexpected help of several royally appointed senators, the leftist and regional parties achieved an unprecedented pro-regional victory by pushing through a proposal to revive the Basques' historical foral rights. PNV representatives, busily condemning the constitutional talks to their constituency, were surprised and elated by the event, calling it a "spectacular novelty."[20]

Shortly after this leftist/regional victory, tensions suddenly shifted. On September 25, a bitter dispute erupted between the Basques and the PSOE when a PNV spokesman, Arzallus, attacked the entire consensual coalition in a speech in Vitoria. Among other things, he said:

> . . . we have no confidence whatsoever in Madrid because we have been under their boot for over a century. Anyone who wants to place his interests there, can choose the UCD, and he who has other peculiar interests, abandoning the interests of his people, can choose among the other parties.[21]

Mesmerized by this attack, Mugica answered for the PSOE:

> . . . this arrogance that pretends to convert the PNV into the expression of Euskadi (the Basque Country) serves to hide the weakness of those who on June 15, 1977 received less popular support than we did . . .[22]

This unexpected twist in the constitution-making process, however, had a fortuitous side-effect for the consensual coalition. It strengthened the somewhat strained PSOE/UCD consensus on the entire constitution. From this point on, the basic consensus between the PSOE, UCD, PCE and MC was cemented. A crucial step in that process was yet to be taken—the approval phase.

The Consensual Approval Phase

Almost entirely dominated by accommodation and expressions of goodwill, the approval phase consisted of four stages. The first stage took place within the joint committee of both houses where eleven representatives swiftly, secretly and consensually put the final touches on the fundamental text. Of the two drafts available, the congressional text was the most successful, especially concerning regional issues. PNV support for the new Constitution was thus risked and, in effect, lost.

The second stage in the approval phase took place on October 31, 1978 when each house separately voted on the adoption of the new Constitution both overwhelmingly supporting it (see Table 3.3). The distribution of the vote reflected the consensual coalition. Excepting one UCD deputy, all UCD, PSOE, MC and PCE members voted affirmatively. In the meantime, five AP and three Basque representatives voted against the constitution and three AP members and twelve Basques abstained (see Tables 3.3 and 3.4).

The third stage of the approval phase consisted of an intense and often heated political campaign geared toward the constitutional referendum scheduled for December 6, 1978. The consensual partners campaigned heavily sending their most prominent leaders around the country to encourage support for the Constitution. The parties at the fringe of the consensus acted more ambivalently. The AP, after much internal bickering and dissension between its more centrist and more rightist members, finally agreed to support the Constitution. Their support, however, was qualified—the AP was quick to point out that it would seek constitutional reform through legislative action. The PNV, disappointed and embittered among other things by last minute changes denying them the broad restoration of foral rights, actively campaigned in favor of abstention.

More extremist parties, excluded from the constitution-making process, recommended abstention or rejection of the text. Both political extremes had ideological reasons for rejecting the Constitution. A stalwart of the extreme right, Piñar, explained that his party, the FN, could not support the new text "because (it) deals a death blow to the essence of Spain: God, the Motherland and Justice."[23]

The third stage of the approval phase came to a conclusion when, on December 6, 1978, the second national referendum in Spain's new democratic history was held. Of the 26,632,180 pool of eligible voters, 67.11 percent cast their vote. Of the 17,873,301 votes cast, 87.87 percent were affirmative. Only 7.83 percent of the voters rejected the Constitution (see Table 3.5). While the national rate of approval was overwhelming, the regional rate of approval differed somewhat from region to region, espcially in the Basque Country. Reasons for the higher Basque abstention rate ranged from discontent to fear of reprisal and violence. Catalonia, historically the most politically radical and progressive of Spanish regions, had a relatively high turnout. But it was in the more conservative geographical areas of Spain, such as Castille, where the highest voter turnouts in the country took place (see Table 4.4).

The approval phase and the entire constitution-making process concluded on a high note. The King signed the Spanish Constitution of 1978 on December 27, 1978. Spain was finally and officially a democracy. The Spanish Constitution of 1978 was thus endorsed by a majority of the Spanish people. Why this endorsement was not heavier is a question many observers have asked. Among reasons cited are the general political passivity of a nation emerging out of forty years of dictatorship. Possible disillusionment with the effectivity of democracy in solving socioeconomic problems may also explain the moderate constitutional interest. The tedious and lengthy nature of the preceding campaign and constitution-making process may also have contributed to some public apathy.

Table 4.4   Spanish Regional Popular Participation in Two
            Post-Franco Referenda

Region	1976 Referendum		1978 Referendum	
	Turnout (%)	Abstention (%)	Turnout (%)	Abstention (%)
Andalusia	81.33	18.77	69.5	30.5
Castile	84.56	15.54	74.0	26.0
Galicia	68.82	31.38	47.7	52.3
Basque Country	58.13	41.87	48.3	51.7
Catalonia	77.72	22.28	68.3	31.7
Canary Islands	75.5	24.4	63.1	36.9
Madrid	78.7	21.3	72.2	27.8
Baleares Islands	82.6	17.4	70.1	29.9

Source: Some information obtained from: Jose Ignacio
Cases, "Resultados y abstencion en el Referendum español de
1978," Revista de Estudios Politicos, No. 6, November-
December 1978, p. 202.

Note: The 1976 Referendum concerned the approval of Prime
Minister Adolfo Suarez's Law for Political Reform; the 1978
Referendum was on the new Constitution.

Conclusions

Several important lessons may be learned from the foregoing analysis. The numerical strength of a political party participating in a constitution-making process should not be the only yardstick with which to measure its abilities. Instead, the strategic placement of a particular party's representatives in the various decision-making bodies (or technical phases) better explains a party's influence on the process. The strategic location of party representatives also determines the parameters of the coalitional game. As long as a party has one or more representatives in the more important committees, it has a reasonable chance of entering into a "winning" coalition such as the UCD/AP coalition and the consensual PSOE/UCD/MC/PCE coalition, the only two consistently successful coalitions of the process.

By tracking the maneuverings of these coalitions through political phases one can obtain an analytical history of the process. This history in turn yields lessons on how constitution-making may succeed. In our examination of the Spanish case several interesting points emerge. It was a very lengthy process often characterized by protracted negotiations and the possibility of breakdown. Such devices as secret negotiations including indirect (non-parliamentary) participants were used frequently and often successfully. The process and the negotiators always aimed at being inclusive rather than exclusive. It was, however, also a process where those who proved inflexible were eventually excluded or ignored. Finally, while popular participation was never direct, the political atmosphere of the nation often had an impact on the development of the process. The foresight of most constitution-makers throughout the process, especially in the face of adverse circumstances (e.g., terrorism), was perhaps their greatest asset.

Notes

1. See discussion in Chapter 3.
2. *El Pais*, 11–12 October 1978.
3. See generally, *El Pais*, and *ABC*, August–November 1977.
4. *El Pais*, 23–27 November 1977, 3 December 1977, 10 December 1977, 7 January 1978 and 11 January 1978.
5. *El Pais*, 7 December 1977, 15 December 1977, 21 December 1977, 24 December 1977 and 28 December 1977.
6. *El Pais*, 6 January 1978.
7. *El Pais*, 2 February 1978 and 21 February 1978.
8. *El Pais*, 25 February 1978 and 8–9 February 1978.
9. *El Pais*, 10–18 March 1978.
10. *El Pais*, 16 March 1978.
11. *El Pais*, 5–11 May 1978.
12. *El Pais*, 21 May 1978.
13. *El Pais*, 24 May 1978.
14. *El Pais*, 8 June 1978.
15. *El Pais*, 12 June 1978.
16. *El Pais*, 8 July 1978 and 12–13 July 1978. Also see, *Cortes: Diario de Sesiones del Congreso de Diputados*, Nos. 106–108, 7 July 1978 and 11–12 July 1978.

17. *El Pais*, 13 July 1978. Also see, *Cortes: Diario de Sesiones del Congreso de Diputados*, No. 108, 12 July 1978.

18. *El Pais*, 22 July 1978.

19. *El Pais*, 12 August 1978 and 24 August 1978. Also see, *Cortes: Diario de Sesiones del Senado*, No. 42, 23 August 1978.

20. *El Pais*, 14–15 September 1978. Also see, *Cortes: Diario de Sesiones del Senado*, Nos. 54–55, 13–14 September 1978.

21. *El Pais*, 26 September 1978. Author's translation.

22. *El Pais*, 26 September 1978. Author's translation.

23. *El Pais*, 17 October 1978. Author's translation.

5

The Political Formula

This and the next chapter explore how the constitution-makers negotiated and compromised on the major parts of the new constitution. Only those articles focusing on the political-governmental machinery of the new regime (the *political formula*) and on the interrelationship between the individual and the state (the *sociogovernmental formula*) are examined. The analysis of each "formula" is twofold. When appropriate, the constitution-makers' evolving positions on given issues are highlighted to demonstrate the effect of compromise. A number of criteria are then applied to the final products of constitutional debate to evaluate their practical value. Such criteria as the relative ambiguity or clarity of the language employed and the constitutionally resolved versus unresolved nature of the issue are used to judge the pragmatic quality of particular articles.

Political formula was briefly defined in Chapter 1 as that part of a constitution that deals with the shape, limits and functions of and interrelationships within the new regime. The political formula thus encompasses constitutional articles defining the new political order and setting up the new governmental machinery which contains both the functional and territorial institutional frameworks. Table 5.1 shows a summary of the constitution-makers' original positions on political formula issues.

Defining the New Political Order

Article 1. (1) Spain is hereby established as a social and democratic state subject to the rule of law. . . . (2) National sovereignty is vested in the Spanish people. . . . (3) The political form of the Spanish State is that of a parliamentary monarchy.

Table 5.1 Initial Positions of Constitution-makers on Political Formula Issues

Issue	Political Actors					
	UCD/Govt.	PSOE	PCE	AP	MC	PNV
Regime Type	Parliamentary Monarchy	Republic	Republic	Parliamentary Monarchy	Republic	Republic
Territorial Organization	Unitary with Regions	Federal State	Federal State	Unitary with no Regional Autonomy	Federal State	Federal State
Role of the Monarch	Representative and Arbiter	Purely Representative	Purely Representative	Representative and Arbiter	Representative	Representative
Cortes Electoral System	Majority System	Proportional Representation	Proportional Representation	Majority System	Proportional Representation	Proportional Representation
Role of Senate	Chamber of Regions & Provinces	Chamber of "Nationalities"	Chamber of "Nationalities"	Chamber of Regions & Provinces	Chamber of "Nationalities"	Chamber of "Nationalities"
Power over Executive	Constructive Motion of Censure	Constructive Motion of Censure	Non-Constructive Motion	Constructive Motion of Censure	Non-Constructive Motion	Non-Constructive Motion
Role of Executive	Preeminent over Cortes	Subject to Cortes	Subject to Cortes	Preeminent over Cortes	Subject to Cortes	Subject to Cortes

Table 5.1 (Continued)

Issue	Political Actors					
	UCD/GOVT.	PSOE	PCE	AP	MC	PNV
Constitutional Reform	Not too Flexible	Not too Flexible	Somewhat Flexible	Demand Flexibility	Not too Flexible	Demand Flexibility
State & Economy	Free Market; Intervention Possible	Intervention & Nationalization Possible	Intervention & Nationalization Possible	Free Market; Protect Private Enterprise	Intervention & Nationalization Possible	Intervention & Nationalization Possible

Note: The brief descriptions provided in this Table are meant to approximate each party's general original position on each issue at the beginning of the constitution-making process; internal party disagreements over what stance to take on any given issue were not unusual, however.

Article 2. The Constitution is based on the indissoluble unity of the
Spanish nation . . . it recognizes and guarantees the right to autonomy
of the nationalities and regions. . . .

Article 6. The political parties are the expression of political pluralism. . . .

Article 9. Citizens and public authorities are bound by the Constitution
and all other legal provisions.

Article 38. Free enterprise is recognized within the framework of a
market economy. . . .[1]

These five articles of the Spanish Constitution of 1978 (hereafter
referred to as the "Constitution") contain the basic definition of the
new regime. The constitution-makers had to overcome several obstacles
to reach the compromise of designating the new regime a *parliamentary
monarchy*. To begin with, there were strong feelings against the monarchical form especially among leftists and republicans, namely the
PSOE, PSP, PCE and most of the regional parties. Their objections
stemmed in part from the fact that Franco had resuscitated the monarchy
through the Seventh Fundamental Law of 1967. The pro-republicans
also argued that the King could not remain a neutral figure. They went
on to point out that today's constitution-makers had no right to impose
the political solution of a hereditary monarchy on future generations.[2]

Partisans of a constitutional monarchy, namely the UCD and the
AP, in return characterized the socialist defense of the republican form
of government as emotionally grounded and unsuitable to modern
political needs. A republic, they argued, was not synonymous with
democracy, and the creation of a constitutional monarchy would achieve
two desirable results: stability through continuity and political change
through popular control of representative bodies. After extensive but
non-confrontational debate, the outcome of deliberations on this issue
was a compromise whereby the pro-republicans conditionally accepted
the parliamentary monarchy. In accepting the parliamentary monarchy,
the socialists recognized the important democratizing role King Juan
Carlos had been playing throughout the transition. The PSOE was also
striving to project a responsible image that would help them gain
governmental stature.[3]

As it was drafted in the Constitution, the role of the King was to
be largely neutral and ritualistic. The King would be:

the Head of State, the symbol of its unity and permanence. He arbitrates
and moderates the regular working of the institutions, assumes the highest
representation of the Spanish State in international relations. . . .[4]

Among the King's moderating functions were his sanctioning and promulgation of laws approved by the legislature and executive. The King was to summon and dissolve the Cortes and call for elections, all under the guidance of the legislature. He was to propose a candidate for president of the government (in Spain the prime minister and the president are one and the same) again only pursuant to instructions from Cortes. If the president requested his presence, the King would preside over meetings of the council of ministers. Among his more symbolic roles were those of awarding distinctions and honors and exercising patronage of the royal academies (of the arts and sciences). Finally, the King was to perform sundry international representative duties.[5]

Among the Monarch's more discretionary powers was his ability to influence the calling of a referendum on a pressing political issue. He was to be, in addition, the supreme commander of the armed forces. The King also had the ability to grant pardons pursuant to the law. The fact that Spain was to be a parliamentary monarchy, however, limited the flexibility of the Monarch in these more discretionary roles.[6]

Defining the regional character of the new regime was as controversial a topic as was the negotiation of the overall territorial formula for Spain. Spain was a nation historically comprised of regions, some of which (namely Catalonia and the Basque Country) had at various times developed forms of self-government. Under Franco all regional distinctions—linguistic, governmental and cultural—had been forcibly removed and fitted into a staunchly unitarian territorial system. Regional groups, namely in Catalonia and the Basque Country, were among the first and most effective democratizing political forces before and during the transition. Their clout, at least regionally, was manifested in their relative electoral success on June 15, 1977.

Few parliamentary groups, except perhaps the AP, truly believed in continuing Franco's extreme form of unitarianism. How to reform this unitarian state, however, became the big question. Parliamentary positions spanned the spectrum. On one extreme were the staunch unitarians, namely within the right wing of AP, among whom were Silva Muñoz, Lopez Rodo and Fernandez de la Mora. Fraga Iribarne, slightly moderating his basically unitarian beliefs, accepted the recognition of diverse regions in Spain but not of nationalities. To the right-of-center, the UCD accepted a degree of regional self-government tied, however, to the indisputable preeminence of the central state. Bunched together toward the center-left and left were the PSOE, PCE and moderate regional groups which espoused various forms of regional self-government to be expressed through "Autonomous Communities." On the other extreme, were hardline nationalistic groups both within Catalonia

and the Basque Country, which would go as far as demanding the
right of regional self-determination.[7]

Given this wide spectrum of territorial-regional positions, compromise became a tortuous enterprise. The regional question was,
without doubt, the stickiest, thorniest and most emotional of all issues
debated. In the end, two parties rejected the constitutional solution:
the AP because it gave regions and nationalities too much independence,
and the PNV because it gave them too little.

The consensual coalition weathered the storm of the territorial negotiations by compromising strenuously. None of the partners of this
coalition was totally satisfied with the final language but nevertheless
accepted it. For definitional purposes, the territorial formula achieved
may be summarized as that of a *regionizable unitary state*.[8]

Defining the economic parameters of the new regime presented fewer
difficulties, although there were some disagreements over limiting the
scope of governmental involvement in the economy. The UCD and
AP advocated the protection of free enterprise and minimal state
intervention in the economy. The remaining constitution-makers supported the option of allowing state nationalization of certain private
industries and state intervention in the economy when deemed necessary.
Under such a constitutional option, a future socialist regime could
legitimately achieve sweeping economic change. Fearing such potential
powers, the more conservative constitution-makers vehemently fought
for the inclusion of clauses protecting free enterprise and the market
economy. Meanwhile, the liberals and leftists advocated the use of such
terms as planning, public initiative and state intervention. The final
constitutional solution included all of these provisions to the overall
satisfaction of most political actors, with the exception of the AP which
maintained its opposition to the possibility of intervention.[9]

Few problems surfaced in the debate over the legal-juridical definition
of the new regime. Given Spain's preceding authoritarian experience,
most if not all constitution-makers agreed that sweeping terms guaranteeing the rule of law and the protection of liberties were necessary.
In Article 1(1) Spain is proclaimed "a social and democratic State of
Law." In Article 9(1), (2) and (3) the supremacy of the Constitution
and of the law over both the state and society is made clear in clauses
guaranteeing the principle of legality and the publication of the law.
In addition, the Constitution provides for the non-retroactivity of
punitive measures that may be adverse to individual freedoms, the
accountability of public authorities and the prohibition of arbitrary
action by such authorities.[10]

In sum, the new Spanish regime, as defined in the Constitution, is
a parliamentary monarchy based on the rule of law, with a regionizable

unitary state and a predominantly capitalist political economy. These constitutional solutions do not reflect the victory of any one political ideology but rather that of compromise. The right-of-center, namely the UCD and the AP, achieved the goal of securing a parliamentary monarchy, of maintaining some form of territorial unity and of protecting free enterprise. Consensual compromise is visible in clauses allowing for the regionalization of the state and the possibility of public intervention in the economy. Ideologically, the parties behaved flexibly, especially the left-of-center in accepting the designation of the state as a parliamentary monarchy. The constitutional language used was largely non-dogmatic and mostly clear and unambiguous.

The New Governmental Machinery

The governmental machinery refers both to permanent institutions, such as the parliament, and to the rules and regulations effecting change within the permanent institutional framework. The analysis of the governmental machinery consists of two parts—the functional balance of power among the various branches of the central state and the territorial balance of power between the central state and the regional and local periphery.

The Functional Balance of Power

Clues about the functional balance of power may be derived from taking a birds-eye view of the Constitution (see Table 5.2). Following the initial listing of "Fundamental Rights and Duties" is the section dealing with the Monarch. The early appearance of this section serves both as a courtesy to the King and to exemplify the "above politics" character of the constitutional Monarch. The fact that the section dedicated to the legislature follows (ahead of the executive) in a political system that is not a republic, alerts the observer to several possibilities. On the one hand, maybe the legislative branch is somewhat preeminent. Or, perhaps its first position in the constitutional order is a concession to certain political forces which, having favored a republic, compromised and accepted the parliamentary monarchy. On the other hand, such a position in the Constitution may be a subtle way of obscuring the actual preeminence of the executive branch. The placing of the judiciary branch at the end of the Constitution remains well within democratic constitutional practice, while the addition of a separate section on the economy and finance, disconnected from the legislature or executive, is somewhat unusual.

Table 5.2 The Spanish Constitution of 1978: An Outline

Title, Chapter and Section			Articles
Preamble			
Preliminary Title			1-9
Title I:	Concerning Fundamental Rights and Duties		10
Chap. I	Concerning Spaniards and Aliens		11-13
Chap. II	Concerning Rights and Duties		14
	Sec. I	Concerning Fundamental Rights & Public Liberties	15-29
	Sec. II	Concerning the Rights & Duties of Citizens	30-38
Chap. III	Concerning the Governing Principles of Economic and Social Policy		39-52
Chap. IV	Concerning the Guaranteeing of Fundamental Rights and Liberties		53-54
Chap. V	Concerning the Suspension of Rights and Liberties		55
Title II:	Concerning the Crown		56-65
Title III:	Concerning the Cortes Generales		
Chap. I	Concerning the Houses		66-80
Chap. II	Concerning the Drafting of Bills		81-92
Chap. III	Concerning International Treaties		93-96

Table 5.2 (Continued)

Title, Chapter and Section		Articles
Title IV:	Concerning the Government and the Administration	97-107
Title V:	Concerning the Relations Between the Government and the Cortes Generales	108-116
Title VI:	Concerning the Judicial Power	117-127
Title VII:	Economy and Finance	128-136
Title VIII:	Concerning the Territorial Organization of the State	
Chap. I	General Principles	137-139
Chap. II	Concerning Local Administration	140-142
Chap. III	Concerning the Autonomous Communities	143-158
Title IX:	Concerning the Constitutional Court	159-165
Title X:	Concerning Constitutional Amendment	166-169
Additional Provisions		1-4
Transitory Provisions		1-9
Repeal Provision		
Final Provision		

Source: Information gathered from: Spanish Constitution 1978 (Madrid: Ministerio de Asuntos Exteriores, Oficina de Información Diplomática, 1979), 122 pp.

The Legislature. Among the more hotly debated issues concerning the legislative branch of government was deciding what type of electoral system to adopt. Supporting a majority system, the UCD and AP sought to avoid the constitutionalization of an electoral law, emphasizing the need for flexibility and citing the successful examples of the United States and the Federal Republic of Germany. They argued that the proportional system would encourage lack of political accountability and would lead toward unstable governments and irresponsible oppositions. Given the broad opposition to the majority system among other constitution-makers, the UCD was eventually forced to accept some aspects of proportional representation. Among the advantages of such representation is its prevention of *caciquismo* in rural areas (and thus electoral fraud) and encouragement of larger, less factional political parties.

Embodying the new electoral system, Article 68 was among the most belabored in the Constitution. It was a compromise between a majority system and proportional representation and consisted of three main points:

- The Congress of Deputies would have a minimum of 300 and up to a maximum of 400 representatives.
- Provinces would be the electoral districts.
- There would be an assigned minimum number of deputies for each province.[11]

This hybrid system was both majoritarian and proportional in that it included a minimum number of deputies from each province while allowing for greater representation in more populated areas. Such an arrangement, needless to say, favored the more sparsely populated, conservative rural interior provinces as they were guaranteed a minimum number of seats in the Congress. In the end, both the UCD and the other partners of the consensual coalition had gotten part of what they had bargained for.

The debate concerning the intra-parliamentary balance of power was not as heated as it could have been. One reason was that the basic parliamentary framework had already been designed during the pre-constitutional period through the Law for Political Reform. In addition, the Congress of Deputies had the upper hand in the constitution-making process per se as it was its subcommittee, congressional committee and plenary sessions that drafted the Preliminary Draft before the Senate had a chance to debate. Most constitution-makers agreed that the Senate, with its territorial representation, would be a useful but secondary body to the Congress of Deputies. Most of the debate concerned what territorial unit the Senate would be representative of. To the regional and leftist parties it was clear that the Senate should be a chamber of the regions and nationalities. To the UCD and the AP this representation had to be based primarily on provinces and only secondarily on regions.

The compromises that followed were again typical of other compromises in this process. While the first paragraph of Article 69 proclaims the Senate the house of territorial representation, such representation was overwhelmingly provincial. There would be four Senators per province, while each Autonomous Community would have the right to "nominate one Senator and a further Senator for each million inhabitants in their respective territories."[12]

Under the Constitution, the Congress kept the upper hand in the drafting of legislation as well. The Senate's influence was limited to that of delaying the approval of bills. Article 90 exemplified the supremacy of the Congress over the Senate. If after two months the Senate did not amend or veto a bill by an absolute majority, the Congress (by a simple majority) could nevertheless submit the bill for the King's signature. On any bill deemed urgent by the Congress, the Senate would only have twenty days to act.[13]

The principle function of the Cortes, as that of any democratic parliament, was that of elaborating and enacting laws. Legislative proposals could be submitted by either the executive, the Congress, the Senate, an Autonomous Community or by popular initiative. The Congress was also given the duty of studying, amending and approving state budgets proposed by the executive. Congressional committees could require the presence of governmental officials to disclose information and report on government policy.[14] Moreover, the Congress would have a limited (constructive) motion of censure which, in cases of legislative unity, would allow it to bring down a government. The censure issue was fiercely debated during the constitution-making process. The most likely governmental parties (the UCD and PSOE) pushed for the constitutionalization of a constructive motion of censure fashioned after the German Basic Law (the German Federal Republic's constitutional law). Such a motion could only be brought at the request of a majority in Congress and only if Congress could simultaneously nominate a new candidate for prime minister. The smaller political parties favored a non-constructive motion of censure that would not require the legislature to find such a candidate. The agreement of the two largest political parties (the PSOE and the UCD) on this issue explains why a constructive motion of censure was so easily constitutionalized.[15]

The Executive. Among the major issues concerning the executive were the creation and termination of governments and the relative strength of the executive within the functional balance of power. Positions on the nomination of candidates for prime minister and the creation of governments ranged from those favoring executive control over the legislature to those advocating legislative predominance. Not surprisingly, the results achieved reflect a compromise of these positions, with the executive branch coming out slightly ahead. The legislature presents the Monarch with its choice for prime minister, and the King in turn officially nominates the candidate. The candidate must then present him or herself to the Congress and spell out his or her political program. Finally, an absolute majority of Congress must approve the candidate. In this scheme of things, the legislature thus seems to have the power of candidate selection, review and approval. The candidate who succeeds, however, has the right to select his or her cabinet after being confirmed thus retaining a critical decision-making power. This somewhat cumbersome arrangement again represents the product of compromise and the dominance of the two major government-minded parties.[16]

The mechanics of terminating governments was another widely debated, but easily resolved, issue. The two major parties again helped each other to achieve mutually satisfactory solutions. Under Article 101, the cessation of governments could take place under four circumstances:

> After the holding of general elections . . . in the event of loss of parliamentary confidence . . . on account of the resignation of the president . . . (or) on account of his [the president's] death.[17]

Three of these four circumstances were easily agreed on with the exception of the termination of a government pursuant to the loss of parliamentary confidence. The constitution-makers were divided between those who sought the constructive motion of censure and those who preferred the non-constructive motion. As before, the UCD and the PSOE were able to handily push through the constructive motion.

In addition to this pro-executive provision, yet another clause favored the executive branch. The government had the ability to present its program to the Congress and ask for a vote of confidence for which only a simple majority was needed. Such a provision gave the government a small but effective tool of self-perpetuation in the face of a potentially hostile legislature. In addition, the president, after deliberating with his council of ministers, could propose the dissolution of the Congress, the Senate or both houses as long as he did so no sooner than one year after a previous dissolution and at a time when no censure motion was underway.[18]

The more mundane aspects of the functioning of the executive branch were easily resolved and generally parallel similar provisions in other western democracies. The government is responsible for directing domestic and foreign policy, the civilian and military administration (bureaucracy) and the defense of the state. Among these duties are maintaining civilian control over the security forces whose "mission" is to protect the "free exercise of rights and liberties and the guaranteeing of the safety of citizens."[19] The government must also see to the economic health of the nation by preparing an appropriate state budget, implementing economic programs and, if necessary, nationalizing key industries.[20]

A final power and responsibility of the executive is its ability to proclaim a state of alarm, a state of emergency and/or a state of siege (martial law). The constitution-makers were again somewhat divided on the state of siege powers. There were those (the UCD and the AP) who advocated the suppression of certain individual rights during such a period. There were others (the PSOE, PCE, PNV and MC) who staunchly defended upholding all individual rights and liberties under any circumstances. In a surprise coalitional victory between the latter parties and three royally appointed senators, a measure protecting all liberties under any circumstance was passed.[21]

The political-ideological behavior of the constitution-makers in dealing with the interrelationship between these two branches of government can be characterized as mostly consensual. None of the participants, including the AP and the PNV, displayed major disagreements with most of the results. The constitutional solutions demonstrate, more than anything else, the victory of the two potential governmental parties, the UCD and PSOE. Their agreement on many of these issues allowed for a relatively smooth compromise and the creation of a parliamentary system somewhat favoring the executive. The constitutional language employed reflects maximum compromise and no ideological dogmatism. The language is largely clear and unambiguous and provides a relatively adequate guideline for practical implementation. Only a handful of issues concerning the functional balance of power were unresolved and left to be decided by a future organic law.[22]

The Judiciary. Confrontations on articles concerning the judiciary were few with the exception of a virulent debate on the degree of its independence from the other branches of government. All parties generally agreed on the need for an independent judicial branch to protect and develop the legal bases of the new democratic regime. They went further to declare, in the first article of Title VI, that "Justice emanates from the people" and is to be governed by principles of independence, irremovability and subjection only to the rule of law.[23]

Two major camps formed among the constitution-makers on the issue of the judiciary's degree of independence. The UCD and the AP advocated the total separation of the judiciary from politics. They argued that in order for justices and magistrates to be beyond political reproach while in judicial office, they would have to sever any political ties they had ever had. The PSOE, PCE, MC and PNV countered with the argument that no citizen, including a justice, could place him or herself above politics or be deprived of the fundamental right of political association. Such a hypocritical requirement, they went on to argue, would in addition endanger the public's right to know the political leanings of a particular judge. The major deliberations on this matter took place in the congressional committee. No real compromise was achieved. The UCD/AP coalition succeeded in pushing through a clause favoring the total separation and independence of the judiciary from politics.

The constitution-makers were otherwise able to agree on the general contours of the judiciary branch. The supreme governing body would be the General Council of the Judiciary comprised of the President of the Supreme Court and twenty members appointed by the King for terms of five years each. The Congress and the Senate would each nominate four candidates for this judiciary body. The Supreme Court would represent the highest judicial decision-making body in Spain— except for constitutional matters, for which a Constitutional Court was set up. The office of Public Prosecutor was created for the purposes of "promoting" justice, the rule of law and citizens' rights. The prosecutor was also to "protect" the independence of the courts and secure through them the satisfaction of social interests. Finally, a public jury system was instituted as well as a judicial police answerable only to judges, the courts and the Public Prosecutor. The actual organizational, bureaucratic and practical details of the new court system were, once again, left to a subsequent organic law.[24]

The functional balance of power formulated in the Spanish Constitution of 1978 therefore displays several characteristics. The King is given a neutral yet moderating role which an adroit individual could put to discretionary use. A balance is struck between the executive and legislative branches of government that can best be described as one of contained competition. The interrelationship of the two branches represents a blend between a republican and a presidential system. Until the president/prime minister achieves office, he is at the mercy of the legislature; once he is confirmed, however, the president has executive powers that go beyond those typical of a purely parliamentary system. The legislature (namely the Congress) still remains a force to be reckoned with, especially in its ability to accept or reject a presidential candidate, hold the government accountable for its policies and pass a motion of censure. Finally, the form given to the judicial branch is a prime example of the effort to disassociate Spain from its arbitrary authoritarian past.

Table 5.3 presents a summary of the major components of the Spanish political formula in the Constitution.

The Territorial Balance of Power

The Constitution-makers and the Territorial Formula. There were two organizational models the constitution-makers could draw upon in their search for the right territorial formula for Spain: the federal and the unitary. Spain's unhappy authoritarian experience with the unitary format, however, meant that something new was needed. Agreement, however, on the contents of such a formula was absent from the very beginning of the deliberations.

The constitution-makers may be grouped into several contingents on this issue. On one extreme of the territorial spectrum was the AP's backing of what bordered on a strictly unitarian state in which regions would be recognized but only nominally within a context largely unchanged from Franco's. Diverging slightly from this position was the initial posture of the UCD. On the one hand, they recognized the historical necessity for greater regional self-management. On the other hand, however, the UCD wanted Spain to remain within a basically unitarian or semi-unitarian structure. Toward the center of the territorial spectrum, were most liberal and leftist parties and moderate regional groups. They backed some form of federalism, akin perhaps to the German Federal Republic, in which regions would have substantial powers of self-government. On the other extreme of this spectrum were the nationalistic regional groups and parties, including the PNV and far more nationalistic groups such as Euzkadiko Ezkerra ("EE"). Their most radical demand was that of allowing regions the right to self-determination (with the concomittant possibility of separation and independence).[25]

Such a variety of territorial positions made reaching a compromise on this issue one of the most difficult tasks of the constitution-making process. Few public signs of disagreement were visible early in the process except for the fact that the PNV was not included in the subcommittee talks. Such an exclusion, however, was due to the PNV's poor showing at the polls (and therefore in the Congress) and was not the consequence of any "undemocratic" practice. The pattern of silence was soon to change, namely when the Preliminary Draft was leaked to the press in November 1977. Once the talks became part of the public record during the constitutional committee deliberations of May 1978, disagreements and emotional arguments on the topic became commonplace. Protracted and tortuous, the debates on the Spanish territorial formula contributed most to the length of the overall process.

Table 5.3 The Spanish Political Formula in the Constitution of 1978

Title	Articles	General Description
Preliminary	1-9	"Political Formula" of the new regime: territorial organization, political pluralism, individual and societal rights & role of the military
Title II	56-65	Role and functions of the Constitutional Monarch
Title III	66-96	Role and functions of the Cortes: Ch. 1 Concerning the two houses Ch. 2 Drafting of bills Ch. 3 International treaties
Title IV	97-107	Role and functions of the executive—government and administration
Title V	108-116	Relationship between the executive and the Cortes, including the constructive motion of censure
Title VI	117-127	Role and functions of the judiciary
Title VII	128-136	Relationship between the state and the economy: government responsibilities and capabilities in a market economy permitting state intervention
Title VIII	137-158	The territorial-regional Formula: the regionizable unitary state
Title IX	159-165	Role and functions of the Constitutional Court
Title X	166-169	Reform and amendment of the Constitution
Additional Provision 8		Promulgation of the Constitution
Repeal Provision		Nullification of Franco's laws and any others contrary to the Constitution

Source: Information gathered from: Spanish Constitution 1978 (Madrid: Ministerio de Asuntos Exteriores, Oficina de Información Diplomática, 1979).

Notwithstanding the highly charged atmosphere in which the territorial debates took place, a thread of compromise ran throughout the process among the parties of the consensual coalition. Flanking this frequently frail consensus were the two habitual non-comformists—the AP and the PNV. The AP never really changed its original pro-unitarian position. The PNV, on the other hand, made several behind the scenes attempts to negotiate and compromise with the consensual coalition. It frequently seemed as if the PNV was about to compromise only suddenly to be met by new demands, often unilaterally concocted by the UCD. At other times, the PNV itself came up with surprise demands thus prompting the breakdown of any incipient agreement. The UCD's behavior on this issue often zig-zagged between holding to its compromises with the coalition and independently reverting to its original, more unitarian position. At one point, the overall viability of the consensual coalition was severely threatened when the UCD pulled such a maneuver during the senatorial committee talks. The UCD announced unilateral changes to provisions concerning the approval of autonomy statutes, the ability of the central state to compete with the regions on cultural and educational matters and the jurisdiction of the Autonomous Community Tribunal. Stunned by this unilateral behavior, the remaining coalitional partners, together with other regional groups, lashed back in virulent senatorial debates. Hopes for a PNV acceptance of both the consensual territorial formula and the entire Constitution began to deteriorate at this point.

An unexpected victory in the Senate among the antagonized coalitional partners and other regional groups followed in the wake of this consensual breakdown. These forces were able to include a provision in the Senate's version of the constitutional draft restoring "foral rights" to the Basque Country. Having won this crucial battle in its overall bid for regional self-government, however, the PNV was once again confronted with renewed UCD demands and a bitter defeat in the joint committee. In reconciling the somewhat different territorial provisions of the Congress and the Senate, the joint committee opted in favor of the congressional version of the issue, which did not include the restoration of foral rights. From this point on, disillusioned and angered, the PNV concentrated its efforts on fomenting popular demonstrations against approval of the Constitution involving, among other things, concerted attacks on the consensual coalitional partners. Such attacks began prior to the conclusion of the Senate's constitutional work in early October 1978 and, curiously, helped to strengthen the consensual coalition. The PNV wound up rejecting the territorial formula and recommending to its followers an abstention on the entire Constitution.[26]

The territorial formula that eventually emerged was a mixed bag of unitarian and quasi-federalistic elements. In Article 2 "the indissoluble unity of the Spanish Nation" is immediately followed by the recognition and guarantee of the "right to autonomy of the nationalities and regions."[27] The system seems to be one that is both unitarian and regionizable. The Spanish state thus becomes an odd hybrid of centralization and potential and selective decentralization. Such a formula can breed regional inequality as it favors regions with strong historical, economic and cultural identities making it difficult for the poorer, less differentiated regions to achieve the autonomous status. Hence, the tag of *regionizable unitary state.*

The Territorial Formula in the Constitution. The core of the territorial formula can be found in Title VIII of the Spanish Constitution. Divided into three chapters—titled "General Principles," "Local Administration" and "the Autonomous Communities"—and twenty-one articles, the formula is built around four territorial units: the municipality, the province, the pre-autonomous region or autonomous community and the central administration. The essence of the formula, however, consists of the interrelationship between the pre-autonomous region, the autonomous community and the central state (see Table 5.4).

There are several ways in which the initiative for autonomy may begin. One option is to initiate the process through provincial councils and "two thirds of the municipalities whose population represents at least the majority of the electorate of each province or island."[28] Such an initiative must be completed within six months. If it is unsuccessful, however, a new attempt may not be started for another five years. A second way to initiate the autonomy process is through the Cortes' adoption of an organic law. A final option is available only to Navarra, where the initiative must emanate from its foral body according to rules spelled out in Transitory Provision number 4.[29]

The routes toward autonomy are therefore few and temporally restricted. The relative difficulty and variability of the process points to a potentially disorganized territorial system in which certain regions attain autonomy quickly, others slowly while some regions never quite make it. Needless to say, the political, economic and administrative repercussions of such a multifaceted system would be a strain on any central and local government.

Once a region attains the autonomous status it gains both rights and obligations. The first and foremost restriction on regional self-government, which "under no circumstances" can be amended, is that the autonomous communities cannot form a federation.[30] They may relate to each other on issues of mutual concern but must always consult with the Cortes in undertaking inter-community agreements. The Autonomous Com-

Table 5.4 Territorial-Regional Issues in the Spanish Constitution of 1978

Title	Articles	General Description
Preliminary	2-4	General statement on the "indissoluble unity of the nation"; recognition of regional differences and the possibility of regional autonomy
Title III	69	The Senate is the legislative body representing provinces and regions; Autonomous Communities may originate legislative initiatives
	87	
Title VIII	137-139	General principles of the territorial organization of the state
	140-142	On local administration: provinces and municipalities
	143-158	On the Autonomous Communities: their creation, regional functions and limitations & relationship with other regional bodies and the central state
Additional Provisions	1,2,3 & 4	On the restoration of historical "foral" rights to certain Autonomous Communities
Transitory Provisions	1-8	Guidelines for provincial autonomy statutes; the initiation of the autonomy process; the special cases of Navarra, Ceuta and Melilla; on the dissolution of autonomous bodies

Source: Information gathered from: Spanish Constitution 1978 (Madrid: Ministerio de Asuntos Exteriores, Oficina de Información Diplomática, 1979).

munity's assembly may draft its own statute of self-government but must remit it to the Cortes for approval. If the statute requires amendment, it must again be sent to Cortes for approval by means of an organic law. Moreover, it is the Cortes that confer upon the Autonomous Community the power to "enact legislation." Cortes may pass an organic law to increase a particular Autonomous Community's powers. The state, through Cortes, may also create laws to harmonize rule-making provisions in the Autonomous Communities.[31]

The Autonomous Community is also subjected to various central government controls. Article 149 lists an exhaustive set of exclusive central state powers. Among its more significant abilities are the state's exclusive jurisdiction over matters of commercial, criminal, procedural, labor, civil, intellectual and industrial legislation. It coordinates all economic planning, finances and state debt. Madrid passes the rules concerning the regulation of the media, the protection of Spain's cultural and artistic heritage and the organization of public safety (i.e., the police). The state in addition bears responsibility for "matters for which jurisdiction has not been assumed by the Statute of Autonomy" and, in cases of conflict with such a statute, the central state's rule is to prevail.[32]

Article 153 spells out the various central state organs to which the Autonomous Community is accountable. Depending on the issue in question, these are the Constitutional Court, the "Government," the central bureaucracy and the Court of Audit. The ultimate expression of the central state's preeminence is embodied in Article 155. In it, the Autonomous Community is cautioned to fulfill its obligations and if it "acts in a way seriously prejudicing the general interests of Spain," the government, after lodging a complaint with the president of the Autonomous Community, may ask an absolute majority of the Senate to support central state measures to force the Autonomous Community to act legally or constitutionally.[33]

Article 148 enumerates the various matters over which the Autonomous Community has some control. Its powers pertain mainly to areas of relative political unimportance such as jurisdiction over recreational ports and airports, agriculture and the raising of livestock, woodlands and forestry, local fairs, handicrafts, museums, libraries and musical conservatories, monuments of interest, the promotion of culture and tourism and of health and hygiene. Among the more substantive areas over which the Autonomous Community has some say are the organization of its own institutions of self-government, the delineation of municipal boundaries, town and country planning, and the promotion of the economic development of the community (but always within the boundaries of national economic policy). According to Article 156, the Autonomous Community can also "enjoy financial autonomy" but cannot unilaterally impose taxes without consulting with the central state treasury. The community may also act "as delegate or collaborator of the State for the collection, management and settlement of . . . tax resources."[34]

The limitations on and powers of the Autonomous Community are thus quite clear. While the Autonomous Community can exercise certain restricted rights and powers, the central state maintains a tight grip on such activities. This relationship may best be summarized by quoting certain phrases from the Constitution. In the article concerning the exclusive jurisdiction of the central state, the first sentence reads: "The State *holds exclusive jurisdiction* over the following matters. . . ." The first sentence of the article dedicated to the jurisdiction of the Autonomous Community says: "The Autonomous Community *may assume jurisdiction* in respect of the following matters. . . . "[35]

The constitution-makers often displayed politically and ideologically charged behavior in negotiating the territorial formula of the Spanish Constitution but in the end most of them settled for a consensual solution. Their compromise was hard won having survived numerous political storms. The parties outside of this coalition remained ideologically rigid, even though in the case of the PNV attempts were made to compromise. Its final rejection of the formula and abstention on the Constitution, however, made the PNV an ultimately inflexible participant in the process. The AP as well may be categorized as an ideologically dogmatic actor on this issue.

None of the constitution-makers was fully satisfied with the final language and solutions achieved. Each of the consensual partners had sacrificed substantial portions of its original position, and none of them expressed great confidence in the formula. Such a lack of confidence had a lot to do with the mediocrity and ambiguity of the formula. Some of the provisions, often filled with superfluous detail, left substantial questions to be resolved by future organic laws.

Conclusions

The Spanish political formula embodied in the Constitution of 1978 may be briefly described as that of a parliamentary monarchy with a regionizable unitary structure. Both the functional and the territorial portions of this formula were largely the result of consensual coalitional negotiations. Most of the constitution-makers were capable, at the end of the process, of accepting (even if with reservations) most of this formula (see Table 5.5).

The portion of the formula concerning the functional balance of power was achieved relatively smoothly, through a strong consensual coalition eventually yielding clear guideline language. The territorial portion of the formula, however, was carved out with difficulty and resolved unsatisfactorily. Confrontation and disagreement characterized most of the territorial talks. Even the consensual partners teetered on the verge of breakdown in negotiating these issues. In the end, the dogmatic positions of the AP, on the one side, and the PNV, on the other, helped to unify the consensual partners into a compromise that eventually succeeded. Unfortunately, the price paid for such heavy compromise was that Spain, a country with relatively intense regional

Table 5.5 The Constitution-makers' Positions on the Political Formula in the 1978 Constitution

Issue	Article(s)	The Parties and Their Final Positions		
		Accept	Accept with Reservations	Reject
Parliamentary Monarchy	1	UCD, AP	PSOE, PCE, MC, PNV	—
Regionizable Unitary State	2, 143-148 & Transitory Provs. 1-8	UCD	PSOE, PCE, MC	AP, PNV
The Monarch as Representative & Arbiter	56-65	UCD, AP	PSOE, PCE, MC, PNV	—
Modified Proportional Representation	66, 68-70	—	All Constitution-makers	—
Senate as a Regional and Provincial Body	69	UCD	PSOE, PCE, MC, AP	PNV
Constructive Censure Motion	112-114	UCD, PSOE	PCE, MC, PNV, AP	—
Slight Pre-eminence of the Executive	97-107 108-116	UCD, PSOE	PCE, MC, PNV, AP	—

Table 5.5 (Continued)

Issue	Article(s)	The Parties and Their Final Positions		
		Accept	Accept with Reservations	Reject
Constitutional Reform: of Articles—Flexible; of Whole—Rigid	166-169	UCD, PSOE, PCE, MC	PNV, AP*	AP*
The State and the Economy: A "Free Market" with Possible State Intervention and Nationalization	128-136	UCD	PSOE, PCE, MC, PNV, AP*	AP*

Note: * On the issues of constitutional reform and state intervention in the economy, the AP's positions often bordered on total rejection. The AP's indecision is attributable to its increasing internal factionalism during the final months of constitution-making. Such internal dissension was namely between the moderate wing of the party, led by Fraga Iribarne, and the more rightist wing led by Silva Muñoz and Fernandez de la Mora.

Source: Author's compilation based on periodical and parliamentary statements and releases. See especially: Cortes: Diario de Sesiones del Congreso de Diputados, Nos. 103-116, 4 July 1978-21 July 1978; Cortes: Diario de Sesiones del Senado, Nos. 39-55, 18 August 1978-14 September 1978; and Cortes: Diario de Sesiones del Senado, Nos. 58-67, 25 September 1978-5 October 1978.

difficulties, was given a poor and incomplete territorial formula with the potential for worsening existing problems. The alternative—a dogmatic territorial solution—would have had the effect, however, of aggravating these problems even further.

Notes

1. *Spanish Constitution 1978* (Madrid: Ministerio de Asuntos Exteriores, Oficina de Informacion Diplomatica, 1979).

2. See generally, *El Pais*, 17–18 August 1977, 30 November 1977, 6 January 1978, 22 January 1978 and 6 May 1978. Also see, *Cortes: Diario de Sesiones del Congreso de Diputados*, No. 59, 5 May 1978, No. 64, 11 May 1978, No. 103, 4 July 1978 and No. 108, 12 July 1978; *Cortes: Diario de Sesiones del Senado*, No. 39, 18 August 1978, No. 47, 31 August 1978, No. 58, 25 September 1978 and No. 62, 29 September 1978.

3. See generally, *Cortes: Diario de Sesiones del Congreso de Diputados*, No. 64, 11 May 1978.

4. *Spanish Constitution 1978*, Article 56.

5. *Spanish Constitution 1978*, Articles 62 and 63.

6. *Spanish Constitution 1978*, Articles 62 and 63.

7. See generally, *El Pais*, 6 January 1978, 18 March 1978, 13 May 1978, 6 June 1978, 17 June 1978, 22 July 1978, 17 October 1978 and 7 November 1978. Also see, *Cortes: Diario de Sesiones del Congreso de Diputados*, No. 59, 11 May 1978.

8. Spain's territorial formula has been described in a multitude of ways; among some of the short-hand terms used are: regional state, state of the autonomies, autonomist state, plural state, federalizable state and federal-regional state.

9. *Spanish Constitution 1978*, Articles 38 and 128. See generally, *Cortes: Diario de Sesiones del Congreso de Diputados*, Nos. 107–108, 11–12 July 1978.

10. *Spanish Constitution 1978*, Articles 1 and 9.

11. *Spanish Constitution 1978*, Article 68.

12. *Spanish Constitution 1978*, Article 69.

13. *Spanish Constitution 1978*, Article 90.

14. *Spanish Constitution 1978*, Articles 66, 87, 134 and 109–111.

15. *Spanish Constitution 1978*, Article 113. See generally, *Cortes: Diario de Sesiones del Congreso de Diputados*, No. 81, 6 June 1978.

16. *Spanish Constitution 1978*, Articles 62(d), 99 and 100.

17. *Spanish Constitution*, Article 101. See Generally, *Cortes: Diario de Sesiones del Congreso de Diputados*, No. 84, 8 June 1978 and No. 109, 13 July 1978; *Cortes: Diario de Sesiones del Senado*, No. 51, 7 September 1978 and No. 63, 30 September 1978.

18. *Spanish Constitution 1978*, Articles 112 and 115.

19. *Spanish Constitution 1978*, Article 104.

20. *Spanish Constitution 1978*, Articles 128–136.

21. See generally, *Cortes: Diario de Sesiones del Congreso de Diputados*, No. 84, 8 June 1978 and No. 109, 13 July 1978; *Cortes: Diario de Sesiones del Senado*, No. 51, 7 September 1978 and No. 63, 30 September 1978.

22. Some of the unresolved issues to be addressed in future organic laws included the organization, duties and principles of the security forces, pursuant to Article 104, and the organization of the council of state, "the supreme consultative organ of the government," pursuant to Article 107. *Spanish Constitution 1978*, Articles 104 and 107.

23. *Spanish Constitution 1978*, Article 117. See generally, *Cortes: Diario de Sesiones del Congreso de Diputados*, Nos. 84–85, 8–9 June 1978 and Nos. 109–110, 13–14 July 1978; *Cortes: Diario de Sesiones del Senado*, Nos. 63–64, 30 September 1978 and 2 October 1978.

24. *Spanish Constitution 1978*, Articles 122–125.

25. See generally, *Cortes: Diario de Sesiones del Congreso de Diputados*, No. 87, 13 June 1978, No. 90, 15 June 1978, No. 91, 16 June 1978, No. 92, 19 June 1978, No. 93, 20 June 1978, No. 112, 18 July 1978, No. 113, 19 July 1978, No. 115, 20 July 1978 and No. 116, 21 July 1978. Also see, *Cortes: Diario de Sesiones del Senado*, Nos. 53–55, 12–14 September 1978 and Nos. 65–67, 3–5 October 1978.

26. See generally, *Cortes: Diario de Sesiones del Senado*, No. 55, 14 September 1978 and Nos. 65–66, 3–4 October 1978. Also see, *El Pais*, 22 and 26 September 1978.

27. *Spanish Constitution 1978*, Article 2.

28. *Spanish Constitution 1978*, Article 143.

29. *Spanish Constitution 1978*, Articles 143–144 and Transitory Provision 4.

30. *Spanish Constitution 1978*, Article 145.

31. *Spanish Constitution 1978*, Articles 145–147 and 150.

32. *Spanish Constitution 1978*, Articles 149, 153 and 155.

33. *Spanish Constitution 1978*, Articles 153 and 155.

34. *Spanish Constitution 1978*, Article 148.

35. *Spanish Constitution*, Articles 149 and 148. Italics mine.

6

The Sociogovernmental Formula

Defining the Sociogovernmental Formula

The sociogovernmental formula describes the constitutionally sanctioned relationship between the state, on the one hand, and society and the individual, on the other hand. Together, the political and sociogovernmental formulas constitute the core elements of a constitution. While the political formula refers to the institutional/functional framework, the sociogovernmental formula contains the rules applicable to the relationship between the state and society/the individual. In a democratic system, such rules are usually well developed, practically implementable (and implemented) and favorable to the individual.

In drafting the sociogovernmental formula, constitution-makers must take into account the protection of individual and societal rights under both "normal" and "extraordinary" circumstances. The drafters must have the forethought of planning adequately for periods of national alarm (states of siege and emergency) without falling into the authoritarian trap of depriving individuals of their fundamental rights. In a nation coming out of a prolonged authoritarian experience, such a task can be challenging, to say the least.

The analysis that follows explores portions of the sociogovernmental under both normal and extraordinary circumstances. In addition, certain relationships between the state and major sociopolitical forces (namely the Catholic Church and the military establishment) are examined. Table 6.1 summarizes the initial positions of the constitution-makers on some of the major issues concerning this formula.

The State and the Individual

Under Normal Circumstances

One of the earliest and easiest agreements among the constitution-makers was to incorporate a full declaration of democratic individual

Table 6.1 Initial Positions of Constitution-makers on Sociogovernmental Formula Issues

Issue	Political Actors					
	UCD/Govt.	PSOE	PCE	AP	MC	PNV
Fundamental Rights & Liberties	Full Declaration	Full Declaration & Additional Guaranties	Full Declaration & Additional Guaranties	Full Declaration	Full Declaration & Additional Guaranties	Full Declaration & Additional Guaranties
Church-State Relations	Maintain Semi-official Relations	Total Separation	Total Separation	Maintain Official Relations	Total Separation	Total Separation
Education	State Support of Private Education; Semi-Secularization	Extend Public Education; Secularization	Extend Public Education; Secularization	State Support of Private Education; No Secularization	Extend Public Education; Secularization	Extend Public Education; Secularization
Abortion	Against	For	For	Against	For	For
Death Penalty	For	Against	Against	For	Against	Against
Divorce	Against	For	For	Against	For	For
Role of the Military	Protector of Constitution Moderator	Protector of Constitution Neutral	Protector of Constitution Neutral	Protector of Constitution Moderator	Protector of Constitution Neutral	Protector of Constitution Neutral
State Emergency Powers	Suspension of Rights Possible	Rights may Never be Suspended	Rights may Never be Suspended	Suspension of Rights Possible	Rights may Never be Suspended	Rights may Never be Suspended

Note: The brief descriptions provided in this Table are approximations. Each party may have had internal disagreement or a variety of views on any given issue.

rights and freedoms into the Constitution. Fashioned after the Universal Declaration of Human Rights and western constitutions, the observance of these fundamental rights would secure one of the pillars of democracy— the protection of the individual from arbitrary authority. The Constitution distinguishes between several groups of rights and duties. First, there are fundamental rights that the state must guarantee. Then there are duties that the individual owes society and the state. Finally, there are provisions for the protection and suspension of individual rights by the state under "extraordinary" circumstances. Parallel to these rights and duties is the fact that the state has the legal monopoly on organized coercion through its control and use of the military and police. For a nation emerging out of authoritarianism these are especially sensitive and important issues.

The Preamble of the Constitution contains several general statements concerning individual rights. The next section of the Constitution, the Preliminary Title, has several further such statements. Article 6, in particular, guarantees political pluralism and participation. Responding no doubt to Franco's "Sindicatos," Article 7 declares the freedom of labor and economic organization. Article 9 proclaims the supremacy of the Constitution and of the law, which are binding on both the state and the individual (see Table 6.2).

It is in Title I, however, that the core of the Constitution's socio-governmental formula lies. Structurally, Title I is divided into five chapters—on the general rights of Spaniards and aliens; on the rights, freedoms and duties of the individual; on the state's socio-economic duties; on the guaranteeing of freedoms; and on the suspension of freedoms. The comprehensiveness with which the constitution-makers treated the subject is unquestionable. In tackling this constitutional area, the drafters seem to have reacted against their nation's authoritarian past.

Clauses on the freedom of religion, education, divorce and abortion were debated at length and were complicated by the extra-parliamentary involvement of the Catholic Church. The Church hierarchy viewed these as issues of morality traditionally within its "jurisdiction." More than anything else, this involvement raised the perennially thorny issue in Spain of the separation of church and state. Other problematic "moral" topics included whether or not to constitutionalize the death penalty, the granting of trade union freedoms and the protection of the individual against arbitrary state power.

The constitution-makers initially formed two camps. The conservatives (the UCD and the AP) stood for the continuation of the death penalty under certain circumstances, the rejection of abortion and divorce (over which the Church would continue to exercise its moral guidance) and

Table 6.2   The Sociogovernmental Formula in the Spanish Constitution of 1978

Title	Articles	General Description
Preliminary	6-9	Political pluralism, participation & trade unions recognized; the military to be regulated; liberty and equality of individuals and groups
Title I	10-38	Fundamental rights & duties: freedom of association, speech, press, religion, political participation & unionization; education; military service; private property; freedom of enterprise; protection of the free market economy
	39-52	List of the government's social, economic & cultural duties toward society
	53-54	The state's guaranty and protection of fundamental rights and duties
	55	Suspension of fundamental rights and duties pursuant to a "state of alarm"
Title II	62	King may call for a referendum
Title III	87	Conditions under which a popular legislative initiative may be pursued
	92	Conditions under which a popular referendum may be called
Title IV	104	Role of security forces: to protect the Constitution and defend the nation
Title VI	118, 125	The individual's obligation to obey the law & duty to participate in the judicial process through the jury system
Title VII	129	Social security rights
Title IX	159-161	Protection of the Constitution in the Constitutional Court

Source: Information gathered from: Spanish Constitution 1978 (Madrid: Ministerio de Asuntos Exteriores, Oficina de Información Diplomática, 1979).

the continued involvement of the Church in education. The other camp, made up of liberals and leftists (namely, the PSOE, PCE, MC and PNV), advocated the abolition of the death penalty, the recognition of abortion and divorce and the strict separation of church and state, especially in the realm of education (see Table 6.1).[1] Given the clearcut differences between these opposing coalitions, intense negotiations were necessary to find broadly acceptable solutions. The liberal camp would have an uphill battle, however, because the UCD/AP coalition had enough clout in the early stages of constitution-making to secure its conservative agenda.

Education. Of these issues, education was perhaps the most complex as it involved decisions on both the overall role of the Catholic Church and of the state in subsidizing and expanding public education. Spain had a history, especially during the Second Republic, of religious conflict between those advocating Church supervision of education and those championing secularization. This conflict was partly due to the inclusion of anti-clerical provisions in the Spanish Constitution of 1931. The constitution-makers of 1978 were well aware of the emotional and sociopolitical implications of the subject. The UCD, more than any other party, had the burden of acting responsibly on this issue. It was largely in its court to decide whether the new Constitution would contain a dogmatic (conservative) or a more pragmatic and broadly acceptable solution. Only the UCD could decide whether to railroad its views into the Constitution through its coalition with the AP or to sacrifice some of its closely held positions in favor of the greater national interest. In the end, the UCD opted in favor of political responsibility and, after much bantering and bargaining, joined in a consensual solution to education.

The solution displayed some of the characteristics of other consensually designed decisions in the Constitution. While the UCD succeeded in inserting a phrase giving parents the right "to ensure that their children receive religious and moral instruction," the liberals, in return, gained provisions expressing their interests such as one proclaiming the "right of everyone to education, through general planning" another allowing teachers, parents and students to "share in the control and management of all the centers maintained by the Administration out of public funds" and yet another asserting "the autonomy of the Universities."[2] Due to its complexity, the article on education became lengthier than necessary and somewhat ambiguous about the degree of Church involvement that would remain. The most important result, however, was that the article was devoid of dogmatic content and basically satisfied most constitution-makers.

Abortion and Divorce. The UCD/AP coalition prevailed on a couple of the other morality issues—namely abortion and divorce. The liberal/left coalition tried to constitutionalize both the right to abortion and to divorce, yet the UCD/AP coalition effectively blocked the inclusion of such resolutions in the Constitution. The only veiled reference to abortion in the Constitution is in Article 15 which states that "all have the right to life and to physical and moral integrity. . . ." The term "all" was used in place of an earlier suggestion that "all persons" be used, thus leaving the door open for future post-constitutional debate on abortion.[3]

Likewise, the only article dealing indirectly with the possibility of divorce leaves that question unanswered. Article 32 reads:

> the law shall regulate the forms of marriage . . . the rights and duties of spouses, the grounds for separation and dissolution and the consequences thereof.[4]

Needless to say, while such an ambiguous statement is not practically helpful, it is still an improvement over the imposition of a one-sided solution as it leaves room for future debate.

The Death Penalty. The one moral issue effectively decided within the Constitution concerned the death penalty. Unlike most provisions in the Constitution, the solution represented a clear victory of the liberal/left coalition which was able to persuade the UCD to join its ranks. The death penalty was abolished "except as provided for by military criminal law in time of war."[5] The UCD once again abandoned the AP in what could have been a certain conservative victory opting instead for a more responsible and widely acceptable consensual solution.

Under Extraordinary Circumstances

The issues dealt with earlier concern the individual and the state during "normal" political times. Some difficulties arose when the constitution-makers discussed the protection of individual rights during extraordinary periods—namely states of emergency, alarm or siege. No one questioned the necessity of a constitutional provision regulating such extraordinary situations. The differences among the constitution-makers were over which individual rights could be curtailed at such times and how deeply.[6]

A coalitional rivalry similar to that concerning the morality issues took shape in this area as well. The conservatives favored curbing the rights of the detained during states of emergency while the liberal/left coalition opposed any such restrictions. Spearheaded by the PNV, measures upholding certain rights of the detained under any circumstances were approved during both plenary sessions of the Congress and the Senate. This represented one of the few instances in which the liberals were able to garner enough support to override a steadfast UCD/AP coalition.

Several further safeguards of individual rights were built into the Constitution. The Constitutional Court would have the ultimate responsibility of protecting the individual through an appeal process involving any individual right contained in Articles 14 through 30, including that of conscientious objection.[7] In addition, the Defender of the People, appointed by the Cortes, would have as his/her prime duty to protect and defend the fundamental rights contained in Title I.[8]

In drafting the articles dealing with these issues, the constitution-makers tried to provide a coherent guideline for action. The results, however, were mixed. They detailed the rights that could be suspended during a state of emergency, alarm or siege. They went on to describe how the various states of emergency must be declared. Particular provisions were drafted to deal with the suspension of the rights of those suspected of participating in terrorist groups and armed bands. Moreover, the drafters noted the importance of counteracting potentially arbitrary state action by including the following language in Article 55:

> unjust or abusive use of the powers recognized in the foregoing organic law shall give rise to criminal liability inasmuch as it is a violation of the rights and liberties recognized by the law.

Unfortunately, however, nowhere in these articles did the constitution-makers define the essence of each state of emergency leaving that and related matters to a future organic law.[9]

The picture that emerges out of this examination is a mixed one. In terms of the coalitional behavior of the constitution-makers, each of the parties in interest got something it had bargained for. The conservatives received concessions concerning the treatment of suspected terrorists. The liberals gained a provision protecting the rights of the detained during exceptional times. The limitations on state power during "normal" times and the limitations on individual freedoms during exceptional times are relatively clearly spelled out. Key ingredients of certain provisions—namely definitions—are missing, however. There is a strong undercurrent throughout the document to guarantee the constitutionality of state action and the protection of the individual, yet an important loophole is left open for future resolution.

The Military Establishment Under the New Constitution

A discussion of the relationship between the state and individual would not be complete without a consideration of the role of the military in the new constitutional order. The constitution-makers agreed on the need to downgrade the political role and independence of the military. How to apoliticize and deprive this entrenched establishment of its powers without instigating retaliation, however, would be a difficult task to accomplish.

At the start of the process, the will to compromise on this subject appeared to be strong among most constitution-makers. It is possible to say in retrospect that among the potentially more volatile issues of the process, that of the military's role was the most easily and smoothly resolved. Even the military establishment, through its top spokesmen, displayed an unexpectedly neutral and supportive attitude toward these constitutional deliberations. Shortly after the Preliminary Draft was leaked to the press, General Gutierrez Mellado, who was both a Senator and the Chairman of the Defense Committee of Congress, expressed the armed forces' support of the evolving constitutional solutions. The draft gave the military the roles of defending the nation, securing its unity and independence and protecting the constitutional order. The armed forces were even willing to accept a constitutional provision allowing conscientious objection to military service.[10]

The constitutional solutions reached within the subcommittee eventually became part of the new Constitution. Little debate on issues concerning the military took place after the first political phase of the process as the remaining constitution-makers generally accepted the language and solutions reached in the subcommittee.

There are three principal articles concerning the military establishment—Article 8 in the Preliminary Title, Article 104 in Title IV "Concerning the Government and Administration," and Article 62 in Title II "Concerning the Crown." Unlike some constitutions which totally ignore the military, the Spanish constitution-makers deliberately referred to the military in the first section of the Constitution:

> The mission of the Armed Forces, comprising the Army, Navy and Air Force, is to guarantee the sovereignty and independence of Spain and to defend her territorial integrity and the Constitutional order.[11]

Except for the second duty, these are functions common to any military corps in a democracy. The second duty, however, confers on the military the ability not only to defend the nation against foreign enemies but also against the enemy within, i.e., terrorists and separatists. Further, the inclusion of an article concerning the military in the Preliminary Title gives that institution a somewhat privileged constitutional position. Article 8 concludes on a vague note with a clause that again postpones certain critical decisions concening the structure and organization of the military to an organic law.

In Article 62 the supreme command of the armed forces is clearly placed in the hands of the Monarch. Such a provision, of course, must be viewed within the context of the Monarch's constitutionally limited role. Article 56(3) unquestionably states that the King's

> acts shall always be countersigned in the manner established in Article 64. Without such countersignature they shall not be valid. . . .[12]

The actual supreme commander of the armed forces therefore turns out to be the president of the government and his competent ministers all of whom are accountable for the King's acts. Thus, in a somewhat circuitous, but perhaps useful way, the armed forces are given both priority in the constitutional order and strict accountability and subjection to legal civilian control.

Further references to the military may be found in Article 28 in which the right of the forces and "other bodies subject to military discipline" to form unions is left to future deliberation. Article 70 forbids "professional soldiers and members of the Security and Police Forces and Corps on active service" from running for deputy or senator in the Cortes. In Article 149(iv) the central state's (rather than the Autonomous Community's) exclusive jurisdiction over defense and the armed forces is inequivocably stated.[13]

Finally, Article 104 concerning the security (police) forces lays down functions similar to those given the armed forces in Article 8. These are mainly to protect the "free exercise of rights and liberties" and to guarantee "the safety of citizens." Again, an organic law is mentioned to determine the "duties, basic principles of action and statute of the Security Forces and Corps."[14]

It is fair to observe that both the constitution-makers and the military establishment demonstrated, if not enthusiasm, at least respect for each other and the consensual solutions achieved. The constitutional text, however, sends mixed signals. While the firm belief in and support for an apolitical, neutral and civilian-dependent military establishment runs through articles on the subject, many of the crucial practical decisions on the implementation of such depoliticization and democratization are left unresolved.

The State and Society in the New Constitution

Church–State Relations

Unlike religious conflict in some other nations, religious tension in Spain has not been between two warring religions but between clerical and anti-clerical (or secular) factions. Political conflict over the official versus unofficial nature of the Catholic Church has existed since at least the early nineteenth century in Spain. Before Franco's overwhelming support for the Church's official involvement in determining Spain's religious, moral and educational fiber, the pendulum had unfortunately swung too far in the opposite direction of anti-clericalism under the Second Republic. The constitution-makers of the Second Republic consciously heightened tensions by including anti-clerical provisions in the Constitution of 1931. Their solutions, as the following excerpts demonstrate, were not only somewhat extremist and dogmatic but also quite negative and intolerant of others' beliefs.

> The Spanish State does not have an official Religion. . . . All Religious confessions will be considered subordinated associations. . . . The State, the regions . . . will not maintain, favor or economically help the churches. . . . Such religious orders as . . . shall be dissolved. . . . The goods of the religious orders can be nationalized. . . . All confessions can exercise their rites privately. The public manifestation of the cult must, in any case, be authorized by the Government.[15]

This list of restrictions on religious institutions and practices in a nation where the overwhelming majority of citizens actively practiced their faith was a provocative and dangerous constitutional move. The events that followed during the Second Republic and the Civil War only attest to the shortsightedness and danger of officially instituting dogmatic, extremist and inflexible decisions on religion in Spain.

The constitution-makers of 1977–1978 had this heavy historical burden to bear in mind as they went about the task of giving Spain an adequate constitutional solution to church-state relations. As was noted earlier, the religious pendulum had swung, under Franco, back toward the full official recognition of the Catholic Church. This status gave the Catholic hierarchy a decisive hand in the formulation and implementation of educational and "morality" policy. Franco, in turn, used the Catholic Church as a tool to fashion the minds of the young according to his moral and ideological wishes.

Such a cozy relationship was, however, not as one-sided as it seemed to be. Within the ranks of the Catholic Church certain developments began to unfold, especially during the last decade of Franco's rule, which would influence the transition. Some of these changes, such as the implementation of Vatican II, were officially sanctioned by the Catholic hierarchy. Other changes, however, developed independently and spontaneously among the younger, more progressive members of the church. Substantial numbers of such progressive clergy actively participated in the democratization of Spain.

Most constitution-makers knew the risks that would be posed by their adoption of one-sided solutions concerning the Church. There were still those who nevertheless espoused monolithic ideas. The AP supported the official recognition of the special status of the Catholic Church that would allow it to continue shaping educational policy and receive state financial aid. Most parties—including the UCD, PCE, MC and PNV—were, however, united in their support of a middle-ground solution in which the state would be secularized and the Catholic Church would be granted a subtle priority among religions and a voice in educational affairs. The PSOE expressed yet another view—it wanted nothing short of a total separation of Church and state and a complete withdrawal of Church involvement in educational policy and of official funding for Catholic Church schools.[16]

The deliberations on this issue became quite tortuous and confrontational. Not only did the PSOE show its discontent (through Peces Barba's withdrawal from the subcommittee in March 1978), but so did the AP once consensual solutions including the PSOE began to take shape. The Catholic Church itself joined as an indirect participant early in the constitutional process shortly after the Preliminary Draft was leaked to the press in November 1977. Its spokesmen were quick to point out the Church's dissatisfaction with several measures. Not surprisingly, the Church's protests centered around provisions secularizing the state and education and introducing the issues of divorce and abortion.[17]

The eventual solutions achieved displayed the kind of ambiguity found frequently in other parts of the Constitution. Article 16 is the principle clause dealing with this subject. In it, freedom of religion and worship are guaranteed without mentioning any religion by name. Next is a statement that reinforces the secularization of the state: "There shall be no State Religion." This wording was carefully chosen to avoid the intolerance associated with Article 3 of the Constitution of the Spanish Second Republic which read: "The Spanish State does not have an Official Religion."[18] A concession to the anti-secularists lurks at the end of Article 16, however:

> The public authorities shall take the religious beliefs of Spanish society into account and shall in consequence maintain appropriate cooperation with the Catholic Church and the other confessions.

The PSOE did not take such an addition lightly, voting against it in the congressional committee. One of the surprising aspects of these talks was that, unlike what might have been expected of it, the PCE was careful to cast its ballot with the centrists instead of the PSOE.[19]

The political-ideological behavior of the constitution-makers on the overall issue of church-state relations was as pragmatic as could have been expected. The PSOE remained dissatisfied with Article 16 arguing that it harbored the subtle confessionality of the state. The AP was, as well, opposed to the solutions reached on education. The other parties (with the general support of the PSOE) were able, however, to achieve a consensual solution. The state would be secular yet could cooperate with religious institutions, among them the Catholic Church. Education was secularized but religious instruction would remain an important subject. On the "moral" issues of abortion and divorce no decisions were made thus relieving the constitution-makers of further obligations. Although not dogmatic (and thereby broadly acceptable), the constitutional language reached on these issues was fairly ambiguous.

Pluralism in the New Constitution

The constitutionalization of pluralism involves the official recognition and protection of one of the pillars of democracy—popular participation. As we have seen, the Catholic Church, no longer an absolutely privileged entity, became one of many groups in the sea of pluralism. Political parties, trade unions, the media/press and universities were among the other major entities explicitly referred to in the Constitution.

The constitution-makers had little argument over including this issue in the text. Some of the details, however, were a little more difficult to settle. There is ample evidence in the Preliminary Title of the general acceptance of pluralism. Article 6 guarantees pluralism through political parties, which are to be the expression of that pluralism and "the fundamental instrument for political participation." Trade unions are given similar treatment in the economic arena through Article 7.[20]

Greater detail on pluralism emerges later in the Constitution. Article 21 addresses the fundamental freedom of peaceful assembly without arms and of demonstrations in public places. In Article 22 the right of association, except in cases classified as criminal, secret or paramilitary, is recognized. Article 23 gives citizens the right to participate in public affairs by voting and running for public office. A somewhat elaborate description of the right "to freely join a trade union" is offered in Article 28 with limitations applicable to members of the armed forces, the security corps and the civil service. The article goes on to recognize the right to strike, with an exception allowing for the maintenance of essential community services. Individuals and groups are, as well, given the right to make individual or collective petitions. Finally, the all-important constitutional safeguard of freedom of expression includes an explicit reference to no prior censorship and to the democratic control, through parliament, of the state media (until recently an authoritarian tool).[21]

The constitution-makers, in addition, weaved a common thread through all of these constitutional references to pluralism by laying down two requirements of all potential sociopolitical entities. First, "their internal structure and operation must be democratic" and, second,

> their creation and the exercise of their activities are free (or shall be unrestricted) insofar as they respect the Constitution and the law.[22]

On the whole, the political-ideological behavior of the constitution-makers on these matters was generally reserved. Sometimes there were protracted arguments, but they were mostly over minor matters or were quickly resolved. The PSOE, for instance, objected to a provision allowing for the creation of private foundations, arguing that it only benefited the wealthy. The liberals and the left objected to the exception concerning "essential community services" during strikes. These provisions were nevertheless passed and, although some hard bargaining took place, the debate over these articles never halted nor threatened to halt the overall process. Most of the constitution-makers expressed satisfaction and acceptance of the articles concerning pluralism. The resulting language was, in addition, fairly clear, undogmatic and implementable.

Conclusion

The Spanish sociogovernmental formula may best be described as comprehensive, moderately conservative and, in some specific respects, incomplete. Unlike other portions of the Constitution, the outcome here was not one of an overall consensual victory but one of limited conservative (UCD/AP) victories tempered by liberal/progressive (PSOE/MC/PCE/PNV) successes. To be sure, several major consensual agreements also emerged—on education and church-state relations. But on certain fundamental right and "morality" issues (abortion, divorce, the rights of detainees), the conservatives managed to squeeze some of their ideas into the Constitution (see Table 6.3). The document, nevertheless, compares favorably to other democratic constitutions' treatment of human rights, containing no glaring omissions or critical ambiguities. Finally, as is common to other parts of this Constitution, the constitution-makers left certain issues open to future elaboration through organic laws. While it is impossible for any constitution to cover all of the practical aspects of an issue, the Spanish constitution-makers did abdicate some responsibility by postponing certain crucial decisions—concerning the military and states of siege and emergency, among them.

Table 6.3 The Constitution-makers' Positions on the Sociogovernmental Formula in the 1978 Constitution

Issue	Article(s)	The Parties and Their Final Positions		
		Accept	Accept with Reservations	Reject
Full Declaration of Fundamental Rights & Duties & Additional Guaranties	10-55	PSOE, PCE, PNV MC	UCD, AP	—
Nominal Separation of Church & State with Special Recognition for the Catholic Church;	16	UCD	PSOE, PCE, MC AP	—
Education: Extension of Public Education; State Subsidies for Private Schools; Semi-Secularization	27	—	UCD, PSOE, PCE MC, PNV	AP
Abortion: Issue Unresolved but "all have right to life"	15	UCD, AP	PSOE, PCE, MC PNV	—
Divorce: Issue Unresolved but Grounds for Separation may allow Possibility	32	—	UCD, PSOE, PCE, MC, PNV	AP
Death Penalty: Abolished	15	PSOE, PCE, PNV MC	UCD	AP
Military: Protector & Defender of Democracy	8, 104	UCD	PSOE, PCE, PNV MC, AP	—

Table 6.3 (Continued)

Issue	Article	The Parties and Their Final Positions		
		Accept	Accept with Reservations	Reject
State of Emergency: State Cannot Suspend All Individual Rights	55	PNV, PSOE, PCE MC	UCD, AP	—

Source: Author's compilation based on periodical and parliamentary statements and releases. See especially: Cortes: Diario de Sesiones del Congreso de Diputados, Nos. 59-93, 5 May 1978-20 June 1978; Cortes: Diario de Sesiones del Congreso de Diputados, Nos. 103-116, 4 July 1978-21 July 1978; Cortes: Diario de Sesiones del Senado, Nos. 39-55, 18 August 1978-14 September 1978; and, Cortes: Diario de Sesiones del Senado, Nos. 58-67, 25 September 1978-5 October 1978.

Notes

1. See generally, *Cortes: Diario de Sesiones del Congreso de Diputados*, Nos. 69–70, 18–19 May 1978, No. 72, 23 May 1978, No. 106–107, 6–7 July 1978 and Nos. 108–109, 11–12 July 1978; *Cortes: Diario de Sesiones del Senado*, Nos. 42–44, 23–25 August 1978, Nos. 45–47, 29–31 August 1978 and Nos. 59–61, 26–28 September 1978.

2. *Spanish Constitution 1978* (Madrid: Ministerio de Asuntos Exteriores, Oficina de Informacion Diplomatica, 1979), Article 27.

3. *Spanish Constitution 1978*, Article 15.

4. *Spanish Constitution 1978*, Article 32.

5. *Spanish Constitution 1978*, Article 15.

6. See materials cited in note 1.

7. *Spanish Constitution 1978*, Article 161(a) and (b).

8. *Spanish Constitution 1978*, Article 54.

9. *Spanish Constitution 1978*, Articles 116 and 55.

10. See generally, *Cortes: Diario de Sesiones del Congreso de Diputados*, No. 67, 16 May 1978 and No., 104, 5 July 1978; *Cortes: Diario de Sesiones del Senado*, No. 41, 21 August 1978 and No. 59, 26 September 1978.

11. *Spanish Constitution 1978*, Article 8.

12. *Spanish Constitution 1978*, Article 56(3).

13. *Spanish Constitution 1978*, Articles 28, 70 and 149(iv).

14. *Spanish Constitution 1978*, Article 8.

15. Author's translation of articles of the Spanish Constitution of 1931 listed in Juan Maria Laboa, *Iglesia y religion en las constituciones españolas* (Madrid: Ediciones Encuentro, 1981), pp. 60–61.

16. See generally, *Cortes: Diario de Sesiones del Congreso de Diputados*, Nos. 69–70, 18–19 May 1978, No. 72, 23 May 1978, No. 106, 7 July 1978 and No. 107, 11 July 1978; *Cortes: Diario de Sesiones del Senado*, Nos. 43–44, 24–25 August 1978 and Nos. 59–60, 26–27 September 1978.

17. For a sampling of the Catholic Church's public pronouncements on the Constitution see generally, *El Pais*, 25–27 November 1977, 3 December 1977, 6 December 1977, 10 December 1977, 3 January 1978, 19–21 May 1978, 7–8 July 1978, 12 July 1978, 22 August 1978 and 28 October 1978.

18. Laboa, p. 60.

19. *Spanish Constitution 1978*, Article 16. Also see, *Cortes: Diario de Sesiones del Congreso de Diputados*, No. 69, 18 May 1978.

20. *Spanish Constitution 1978*, Articles 6 and 7.

21. See respectively, Articles 21, 23, 28, 29, 34, 36, and 52 in *Spanish Constitution 1978*. See generally, for deliberations concerning (1) pluralism and political parties: *Cortes: Diario de Sesiones del Congreso de Diputados*, No. 67, 16 May 1978 and No. 104, 5 July 1978 and *Cortes: Diario de Sesiones del Senado*, No. 41, 22 August 1978 and No. 59, 26 September 1978; (2) trade unions and employer associations: references in (1) above and *Cortes: Diario de Sesiones del Congreso de Diputados*, No. 72, 23 May 1978, No. 107, 11 July 1978 and *Cortes: Diario de Sesiones del Senado*, No. 45, 29 August 1978 and

No. 61, 28 September 1978; and (3) freedom of expression and communication: *Cortes: Diario de Sesiones del Congreso de Diputados*, No. 70, 19 May 1978 and No. 106, 7 July 1978 and *Cortes: Diario de Sesiones del Senado*, No. 43, 24 August 1978 and No. 106, 27 September 1978.

22. See Articles 6, 7, 36 and 52 in the *Spanish Constitution 1978*.

Part 3

7

The Spanish Experience
in Comparative Perspective

Introduction

In this chapter, several cases of constitution-making during transitions to democracy will be briefly compared to the Spanish experience of the late 1970s. Although such a comparison would be more useful if in-depth case studies existed, it is nevertheless worthwhile to compare the Spanish Second Republic, postwar Germany and Italy, and contemporary Portugal to present-day Spain.

The Comparative Case Studies

The mini-case studies profiled in this chapter share a number of features with contemporary Spain. No third world nations have been included as their authoritarian experiences are often rooted in some form of colonialism or foreign dependence. In all cases, a prolonged and profound period of authoritarian rule preceded the transition. In each case, a democratic regime, lasting for at least five years, emerged out of a completed constitution-making process.

Spain (1931). The Spanish transition to democracy of 1931, which led up to the ill-fated Second Republic, is one of the mini-case studies. Preceded by the eight-year dictatorship of General Primo de Rivera, the transition, including the constitution-making process, lasted a brief six months. Nearly five turbulent years of democracy followed only to end in the Spanish Civil War of 1936–1939.[1]

Italy. The Italian transition to democracy was a product of both authoritarian regime breakdown and military defeat. Disenchantment and opposition to Mussolini's lengthy rule alone may not have allowed for a successful turning point toward democratization. A peculiar and essential ingredient in that turning point was the dictator's losing military effort in World War Two. Although plagued by countless governmental change-overs, the democratic regime founded in the late 1940s has survived almost intact to this day.[2]

Portugal. Preceding the contemporary Spanish transition by a couple of years was the Portuguese experience. Portugal shared with Spain the backdrop of an entrenched and long-lived authoritarian regime which had lasted over forty years. The Portuguese turning point toward democratization differed substantially from that of Spain, however. An unusual group—the military—spearheaded internal opposition to the dictatorship. Trouble in Portugal's disintegrating African colonies provided the military and the nation with a focal point for anti-authoritarian activities. The democracy born out of such disintegration has nevertheless survived through a somewhat turbulent decade.[3]

Germany. The final case is somewhat unusual—that of Germany after World War Two. Although the external defeat of the totalitarian Nazi regime provided circumstances conducive to a turning point toward democratization, the German constitution-making process and outcome have proven to be among the most successful of the twentieth century. Few, if any, other cases of totalitarian regime transition to democracy have ever taken place. Indeed if such a transition is possible, it could only take place as a consequence of external military defeat and the imposition of democracy or after the existence of an intermediate authoritarian period. The German Basic Law (as its constitution is named) is today one of the leading models of a democratic constitution emulated, among others, by the Spanish constitution-makers of 1977–78.[4]

A Brief Comparison of Germany and Spain. Germany and Spain share some intriguing historical similarities. In the early twentieth century each country experienced novel and unrestrained forms of republican government—the Weimar Republic and the Second Republic. In both instances, there were constitution-making processes and outcomes that deeply and dangerously affected the workings of the new regimes.

Lasting from 1918 to 1931, the Weimar Republic followed a substantial period of authoritarian rule (first under Bismark and then under King Wilhelm) and external defeat during World War One. The Weimar constitution-making process was very much a reaction to the authoritarian past. Democratic constitution-making was a somewhat novel art even though successful historical cases existed—in the United States and the various French Republics. The German constitution-making process was especially experimental in that new and different social conditions were developing in the early twentieth century. Among these was the advent of mass political participation and ideological mobilization through political parties and trade unions.

The Weimar constitution-makers, unrestrained in their democratizing euphoria, unfortunately overlooked certain necessary democratic safeguards. One of the major mistakes of the Weimar Constitution, with a subsequently devastating effect on the survival of the republic, was its treatment of the relationship between the presidency and the parliament (Reichstag). The constitution legitimized a duality of top decision-making roles—that of the president and that of the chancellor, the head of the legislature—so that the former had the ability to govern by decree. Such a provision gave the president the almost unfettered power to dissolve parliament and call for new elections at will. Abuses and manipulations of these provisions inevitably developed, especially when Adolph Hitler was elected Chancellor. The constitution thus aided Hitler in his rise to total power as he seized the reigns of power from a weak president (Hindenburg).[5]

Spanish political history in the early twentieth century offers some interesting parallels to the German experience. Dominated by leftists and liberals, the constitution-making process preceding the Second Republic was swift and unrestrained. The leftists' ideological zealotry and majority status in the process helped them to achieve dogmatic constitutional solutions. Chief among these tainted provisions were a series of articles providing for the total separation of church and state and, to an extent, the persecution and punishment (through confiscations, e.g.) of the Catholic Church. Such a one-sided solution to a divisive and emotional issue contributed substantially to the breakdown of the Second Republic five years after its inception. As in the German case, the imposition of an ideological constitution in a weak democracy plagued by profound domestic problems could only hasten its disintegration.

Although subsequent German and Spanish experiences differ substantially, there are still certain unusual similarities. Unlike some of his contemporaries, Franco was shrewd enough not to become directly and openly involved in World War Two. Needless to say, Franco may have secured himself a lengthy stay in Spanish politics because of such a move. Undoubtedly, Germany, Italy and Japan's involvement and defeat in World War Two helped to destroy those countries' respective totalitarian or authoritarian regimes. While Germany under Hitler underwent twelve years of totalitarian control, Franco's authoritarian rule lasted thirty-six years. Although for different reasons, successful transitions to democracy followed the deaths of Hitler and Franco. What is most interesting about both of these transitions is that their constitution-making efforts display dramatic similarities both in process and outcome.

The Constitution-making Process in Comparative Perspective

Turning Points Toward Democratization

Spain (1931) and Portugal. The Spanish and Portuguese transitions were possible because in each instance there was a simultaneous decline of authoritarian rule and emergence of sociopolitical pluralization. The role of each nation's military was also critical in allowing the peaceful transfer of power to new democratic elites. The Spanish military was disenchanted with Primo de Rivera's ineffective rule and the passivity of a weak monarch, Alfonso XIII. The Portuguese authoritarian regime's inept and costly handling of its disintegrating African colonial empire was its military's chief source of disaffection. In each case, the confluence of regime breakdown and sociopolitical pluralization spearheaded by a pro-democratic (or, at least, neutral) military made turning points toward democratization possible.

Germany and Italy. Postwar Italy and Germany exhibit a second set of factors allowing for a turning point toward democratization. External military defeat and the imposition of democratization by victorious allied forces were the necessary ingredients in both cases. In Italy, unlike Germany, there had been a substantial underground opposition to the authoritarian regime during the war. The leaders of these forces were well suited to the task of building Italy's new democracy. Because of the existence of this fairly well developed internal opposition, Italy had a substantial pluralization at the beginning of its transition to democracy. The Italian sociopolitical realities allowed for a more independent and unsupervised transition and constitution-making process than that possible in Germany at the time.

No real opposition to Hitler had developed within German borders during the war although a small but ineffective exiled group had lived in Scandinavia. This group, together with other younger, pro-democratic leaders, would become the cream of the new German political elite. Their democratizing steps, however, were under strict allied supervision since the defeated German nation's primary features were political passivity and the absence of effective pluralization.

Contemporary Spain. A third and final set of factors explain the Spanish turning point toward democracy of the late 1970s. Key among these factors were a well developed and organized sociopolitical pluralization, and the choice, by what appeared to be authoritarian elites, of political reform. Reform initially meant reform within the regime, yet the existence of well-placed "authoritarian" elites with democratic objectives—King Juan Carlos and Prime Minister Adolfo Suarez—transformed mere internal reform into reform with regime change.

Comparative Turning Points. Based on these examples, there are at least three possible turning points towards democratization. In some cases, the authoritarian regime disintegrates (the elite loses control or dies), and there is active sociopolitical pluralization and critical pro-democratic military encouragement (or neutrality). In other cases, the authoritarian (or totalitarian) regime is defeated at war, the external victors encourage democratization and capable domestic elites take charge. A third type of turning point occurs when authoritarian "auto-ruptura" takes place and previously excluded democratic elites, supported by broad sociopolitical pluralization, begin to participate in political life.

The Constitution-makers and Their Coalitions

A variety of political forces usually emerge out of a successful turning point. Among the first democratic political activities to face these groups is some form of nationwide election to decide the initial distribution of political power in the country. In each of the cases profiled, with the exception of Germany, such elections were high on the nation's agenda. Since one of the main purposes of early elections is the formation of a constitution-making entity, their impact on the political and ideological composition of such an entity is decisive.

Spain (1931). The socialists (PSOE), radicals and radical socialists (together, the republican left) were the clear victors in the Spanish elections of 1931. These parties went on to form a dominant majority coalition in Cortes which enabled them successfully to push through a leftist constitution (see Table 7.1).

Italy. The Italian elections of June 1946 gave the DC (christian democrats of center-right persuasion) the greatest number of votes. A substantial socialist and communist contingent followed. Together these two parties could have formed a majority leftist coalition. Instead, fluid and fluctuating coalitions were the name of the Italian constitution-making game. Clearly, such flexible coalitional behavior among parties with widely differing ideologies laid the groundwork for the constitution of compromise—rather than dogmatism—that resulted (see Table 7.1).

Germany. The allied forces were not too quick to restore political autonomy to the German elite. Indeed, a somewhat unusual pre-constitutional process preceded the full implementation of democracy in Germany. Elections were not held for a constituent assembly. Instead, state legislatures ("Landtage"), never too far from allied supervision, appointed members to the "Parliamentary Council" that became the constitution-making body. These members represented the major democratic parties in Germany at the time. Among the parties with most

Table 7.1 Comparative Party Representation in Several Constitution-making Bodies

Spain 1931 (469 Seats)		Italy 1946 (555 Seats)		Germany 1949 (65 Seats)		Portugal 1976 (247 Seats)		Spain 1977 (350 Seats)	
Socialists & Republican Left	257	Christian Demo.	207	CDU/CSU	27	PS/Socialists	115	UCD	165
		Socialists	115	SPD	27	PPD/Center	80	PSOE	118
Center, Agrarians & Independents	158	PCI/Communists	104	FDP/Liberal Democrats	5	PCP/Communists	30	PCE	20
		Other Center & Center Left	64	Center/Right	2	Other Center Right & Right	16	AP	16
Center Right, & Right	54	Other Center Right & Right	30	Center	2	Other Center Left & Left	6	CC	13
		Other	35	Communists	2			PNV	8
								Other	10

Sources: The data for this Table (other than that for Spain in 1977) was obtained from the following sources: (1) Spain 1931: Juan J. Linz, "From Great Hopes to Civil War: The Breakdown of Democracy in Spain", in The Breakdown of Democratic Regimes: Europe, Juan J. Linz and Alfred Stepan, eds. (Baltimore, Maryland: The Johns Hopkins University Press, 1978), pp. 146-48; (2) Italy 1947: Raphael Zariski, Italy: The Politics of Uneven Development (Hinsdale, Illinois: The Dryden Press, Inc. 1972), pp. 156-57; (3) Germany 1949: Peter H. Merkl, The Origins of the West German Republic (New York: Oxford University Press, 1963), pp. 58-60; and, (4) Portugal 1976: Richard Robinson, Contemporary Portugal (London: George Allen & Unwin, 1979), p. 235.

delegates to the constitutional talks were the CDU/CSU (christian democrats of center-right persuasion) and the SPD (social democrats, of liberal and leftist tendencies), followed by the coalitionally important FDP (free democrats with a moderate/centrist perspective). Most constitutional provisions were hammered out by a three-way consensus coalition, although on certain issues the SPD opposed the more conservative solutions achieved by a majority CDU/CSU-FDP coalition (see Table 7.1).

Portugal. Portugal in the 1970s is a case that closely parallels Spain in 1931. Leading in the popular vote, the socialist party (PS) achieved predominance in the constitution-making process. With the close assistance of the radicalized military, the PS was able to achieve a somewhat dogmatic (leftist) constitution over the heads of the more centrist, second largest party, the People's Democratic Party (PPD) (see Table 7.1).

Contemporary Spain. The coalitions resulting from the elections of 1977 were not strictly ideologically one-sided. In fact, the prevailing coalition—the consensus coalition—contained a variety of ideological viewpoints. The only other effective coalition (the conservative UCD/AP coalition) was intermittent at best in its successes, never dominating any of the political phases of the process (see Table 7.1).

Comparative Constitution-making Coalitions. The first post-turning point elections in a nation undergoing a transition to democracy are crucial. As a result of such elections, the ideological and coalitional parameters of the constitution-making process are set. In Spain (1931) and Portugal, the predominant party was leftist and coalesced with forces of similar ideological persuasion, enabling them to craft a dogmatic (leftist) constitution. In Italy and contemporary Spain and (to a lesser extent) Germany, the predominant centrist political force—the DC, UCD or CDU/CSU respectively—formed intermittent coalitions with the main opposition parties—communists and socialists in Italy, socialists and regional parties in Spain and social democrats and free democrats in Germany. The results in each case, as will be seen later in this chapter, were non-dogmatic constitutions.

From this brief overview of parties and coalitions involved in the various constitution-making processes, it is possible to make several observations. When a political party situated on either end of the political spectrum achieves a clear electoral majority prior to the constitution-making process, it will have a strong urge to pursue an ideologically one-sided political route (e.g., Portugal). A similar process may result from the coalition between two or more ideologically compatible parties of either extreme (e.g., Spain in 1931). Such a development does not augur well for the future of that democracy because other parties, leaders and substantial sections of society will continue to oppose the one-sided solutions. The political consequences of such dogmatic constitutions can be severe as the case of the breakdown of the Spanish Second Republic makes clear. When a moderate or centrist political party either achieves an electoral majority or through coalitions attains such a status, the pressure to write an ideologically balanced (or non-ideological) constitution will be far greater (e.g., Italy, Germany and contemporary Spain). It seems clear that in cases in which pre-constitutional elections yield ideologically one-sided results, the victors must exercise a great deal of political responsibility if they want to avoid the perils of imposing dogmatic solutions on the nation.

The Political Phases in Comparative Perspective

There are two main criteria that distinguish the political phases of a constitution-making process—the prevalence of consensual or dissensual modes of decision-making and the ideological breadth or narrowness of the dominant coalition(s). In Spain, six political phases were distinguished. Out of the six phases, only one was totally dissensual (the "Dissensual pre-Congressional Phase") insofar as it displayed confrontational decision-making and an ideologically one-sided dominant coalition (the UCD/AP). In the other five phases, including the most difficult one—the "Constrained Parliamentary Phase"—accommodational decision-making prevailed. Moreover, the dominant coalition throughout these phases—the consensus coalition—represented a broad integration of diverse political partners ranging from the center-right (the UCD) to the clear left (PCE) and the regions (MC).

What follows is an attempt to compare the Spanish contemporary experience to that of the other four cases. The comparison is by no means rigorous since this book has focused on one transition and because comparable findings for the other examples could only be reached through case studies similar to the one undertaken here. This general comparison is nevertheless useful because it underscores the main differences and similarities between these cases.

Spain (1931). The Spanish Constitution of 1931 was drafted relatively quickly (in six months) by a dominant leftist coalition. The sociopolitical setting was not entirely peaceful as Spain faced deep social, regional and economic problems, and the leaders of the winning coalition did not squarely face the potential dangers of dogmatism. Instead of consulting with parties of different persuasions, the coalition pushed through a series of constitutional measures guaranteed to exacerbate some of the severe religious and economic divisions in the country. Among such measures was the rash decision to separate church and state in a nation where the overwhelming majority of citizens were practicing Catholics.

The constitutional provisions governing such a separation were, in addition, written in offensive and inflammatory language. The coalition also introduced measures to reform and reduce the powers of the military which had just contributed to the successful turning point toward democratization. Pro-regional measures were approved to allow certain regions, namely the Basque Country and Catalonia, to achieve greater forms of self-government. Strong pro-labor measures were introduced in a country where rich industrialists and large landowners had long been favored.[6]

The Second Republic was thus born out of an almost completely polarized process—a process dominated by a leftist coalition that never truly compromised with any party of a different ideological outlook. Such unilateral and confrontational decision-making coupled with its foreseeable results—an ideological constitution—in a nation with deep political, religious and economic polarization could only contribute to the eventual demise of democracy.

Italy. The Italian electoral results, giving the DC an edge but providing the socialists and communists with a potential coalitional majority, seemed to work in favor of centripetal, consensual constitution-making. No one coalition dominated Italian constitution-making. Instead, fluid coalitions and consensual decision-making took place on an issue-by-issue basis. Among the dilemmas confronting these constitution-makers were whether or not to resuscitate the (pre-Mussolini) monarchy or to create a republic, and how to reduce deep north-south economic inequalities. Even in the face of these potentially divisive issues, the process developed and was completed on a consensual basis with most, if not all, political parties supporting the final version of the new constitution.[7]

Germany. The German case is unique. No constituent assembly or directly elected body drafted the constitution. A very special responsibility rested with those selected to draft the new "Basic Law." Germany and its political behavior were under collective allied microscope. Consensual decision-making and non-ideological solutions would thus have to be the unwritten guiding principles of the process. While the CDU/CSU maintained a slightly predominant position in the process and its negotiations (frequently joining the FDP to counter the views of the SPD), coalitions were fluid and frequently included the SPD. Indeed, the only unusual and sometimes disruptive factor present in the process was that of unnecessary allied supervision. The German constitution-makers nevertheless dominated the process, which was completed in a little over nine months. The character of decision-making was largely accommodational and multilateral and the nature of the predominant coalitions was never strictly ideological. The German Basic

Law became a model of effective compromise displaying both pragmatism and clarity.[8]

Portugal. The Portuguese case again parallels that of Spain in 1931. The socialists, with the aid of other leftist parties (namely the radical communist party, the PCP), achieved a majority in the constituent assembly and went on to pursue ideological constitutional solutions. The drafting was a relatively slow process (one year) and yielded a copious number of articles—312. Many of these articles, especially those regarding agriculture and landlord-peasant relations, were clearly ideological and often purely rhetorical. Dogmatic language is already patent in the Preamble of the Portuguese Constitution of 1976:

> ... The liberation of Portugal from dictatorship, oppression and colonialism represented a revolutionary change and an historic new beginning in Portuguese society. The Revolution restored fundamental rights and freedoms to the people of Portugal. ... The Constituent Assembly affirms the Portuguese people's decision ... to secure the primacy of the rule of law in a democratic state and open the way to a socialist society. ...[9]

Obviously, parts of this preamble and of the remainder of the constitution did not represent the opinion of all Portuguese people, including those associated with the second most popular party, the centrist PPD which had received 26.4% of the 1975 vote. While most parties expressed their "respect" for the new constitution when it was approved, one of the centrist parties, the CDS (Party of the Social Democratic Center), voted against it.

A peculiar influence on the Portuguese Constitution was that of the armed forces, which played a central role in bringing about the turning point toward democratization and thus occupied a favored position in Portuguese society. Such "favor" was translated into a special constitutional role for the military that can best be described as that of an arbiter, "above politics," with the potential for decisive discretionary power.[10]

While the Portuguese constitution-making process was not one that displayed the intense polarization evident in the Spanish case of 1931, it was nevertheless a dissensual process. Decision-making, coalitions and results were ideologically one-sided and achieved unilaterally. The process may, however, be generally characterized as passively dissensual in that it lacked the aforementioned polarization.

Comparative Political Phases. Unless the party achieving electoral predominance also attains an absolute majority in parliament, it can pursue a variety of coalitional strategies. If this party is located on one of the two political extremes, it can draw upon smaller parties of similar ideological persuasion. Such an ideologically one-sided strategy usually yields unilateral constitutional decision-making and, eventually, a dogmatic constitution. Depending on the severity of social, economic and/ or political problems present in the country at the time, such dissensual constitution-making may have dangerous consequences for the effective functioning of the new democracy. The dissensual process may be either active with a decisive impact on the new regime's long-term survival (e.g., Spain 1931) or passive with unclear and perhaps indirect consequences on the functioning of the new regime (e.g., Portugal). Where there is active opposition to the dominant coalition during a dissensual constitution-making process, there is likely to be continued post-constitutional opposition. Such post-constitutional opposition may be weaker or non-existent in the case of a passively dissensual constitution-making process.

A predominant extremist party can, however, pursue a more conservative coalitional strategy—that of coalescing with a smaller moderate party(ies) or a party(ies) on the opposite side of the spectrum. If such a strategy does not break down in midstream, it can only lead to a more balanced, accommodational and multilateral decision-making process and a constitutional outcome that will not antagonize or polarize significant segments of the nation.

When the predominant party is moderate or centrist it will probably seek a coalition with the second (and/or third) most popular parties (further to the right or left). The fact that such a majority coalition will have both a centrist core and some ideological representation will allow for multilateral decision-making and fewer dogmatic solutions. The overall constitution-making process may have a better chance of being consensual although dissensual situations and phases are possible (as we saw in the case of Spain 1977–78). The resulting constitution may contain ideological sections but will not be so in its entirety. Such results can only bode well for the emerging democracy as major parties (and the social sectors they represent) are not excluded from the process. The examination of the Italian, German and Spanish (1978) cases would seem to confirm these observations.

The Constitutional Formulas in Comparative Perspective

As was seen in Chapters 5 and 6, the examination of a constitution's political and sociogovernmental formulas involves both an analysis of the negotiating behavior of the constitution-makers (accommodational or confrontational, unilateral or multilateral) and of the actual language (dogmatic or non-dogmatic, practical or rhetorical) resulting from their negotiations. The analysis of the political formula is twofold, consisting of an examination of the functional balance of power and of the territorial balance of power. The sociogovernmental formula concerns the relationship between the state and the individual on the one hand, and the state and society on the other hand.

The Political Formula in Comparative Perspective

In Chapter 5, the Spanish constitution-makers' behavior concerning the functional balance of power was found to be largely consensual, with accommodation and multilateral decision-making prevailing. Most, if not all, provisions governing the state's internal institutional make-up were neutral and undogmatic, providing relatively clear guidelines for political action.

There were several problems concerning the formulation of the territorial balance of power, however. The constitution-makers often displayed dissensual behavior marked by polarized coalitions—with liberals and leftists forming a pro-regional coalition and conservatives forming a pro-unitary coalition. Facing such polarization among themselves, the parties of the consensual coalition strained to reach territorial compromise, eventually succeeding. The parties outside the coalition, namely the AP and the PNV, maintained their original positions in a steadfast and, in the end, uncompromising fashion.

The resulting territorial language reflected some of these problems. While it was the result of compromise and thus largely undogmatic, the text generally favored conservatives in its support of the supremacy of the central state. The length and ambiguity of much of the text was a second major problem making the successful implementation of the territorial provision difficult at best. Finally, the often unresolved nature of many of the territorial provisions only underscored the possibility of future conflict over the territorial character of the Spanish state. The essence of the new regime's political formula might best be summarized as that of a parliamentary monarchy with a regionizable territorial structure.

It is impossible to review the mini-case studies presented here as substantively as the contemporary Spanish case. It is possible, however, to scratch the surface of each of these cases by summarizing the coalitional behavior of each nation's constitution-makers and the content of each constitution's political formula.

Spain 1931. One of the major problems of the Spanish process of 1931 was the almost total absence of compromise throughout the process. A dominant leftist coalition maintained control, forcing its ideological constitutional platform on the nation. The resulting language was not only dogmatic but frequently provocative to those holding other views.

Table 7.2 Outline of the Spanish Constitution of 1931

Preliminary General Provisions
- I. National Organization
- II. Nationality
- III. Rights & Duties of Spaniards
  - 1. Individual & Political Guaranties
  - 2. Family, Economy & Culture
- IV. The Cortes
- V. Presidency of the Republic
- VI. Government
- VII. Justice
- VIII. Public Finance
- IX. Guaranties & Reform of the Constitution

Source: Author's translation of information contained in: Miguel Martinez Cuadrado, "La Constitucion española de 1978 en la historia del constitucionalismo español," in La Constitucion española de 1978: estudio sistematico, Alberto Predieri and Eduardo Garcia de Enterria, eds. (Madrid: Editorial Civitas, S. A., 1981), p. 38.

The political formula of the Spanish Constitution of 1931 created a republic over the objections of those (including the military) who favored continuing some form of monarchical presence. The constitution-makers created a dominant legislative branch that could exert clear control over the executive. Provisions concerning the creation and termination of governments were conducive to instability allowing, for instance, for non-constructive votes of no confidence. The territorial portion of the political formula provided, in turn, for relatively broad forms of self-government to a select few regions, namely the Basque Country and Catalonia.

Between the dissensual character of the process and the dogmatic content of such key provisions of the political formula, the emerging regime had an added burden in its attempts to govern the nation and resolve its problems peacefully. While the governments comprising the Spanish Second Republic did not use violence to implement their goals, the unfortunate legacy of the constitution added to the nation's deep domestic problems. The governments' inability to cope ultimately ended in violence often instigated by those originally excluded from constitution-making—the right and the military (see Table 7.2).[11]

Table 7.3 Outline of the Italian Constitution of 1947

> Basic Principles
> I.   Rights & Duties of Citizens
> II. Organization of the Republic
>   Parliament
>   President
>   Government
>   Judiciary
>   Regions, Provinces & Municipalities
>   Constitutional Guaranties
>   Transitory & Final Provisions

Source: The Constitution of the Republic of Italy
(Rome: Chamber of Deputies and Senate of the
Republic, 1979).

Italy. In 1947, the Italians confronted a question similar to that in Spain in 1931—whether to allow the restoration of a monarchical form of government or to pursue a strictly republican regime. The breadth of ideological representation in the prevailing constitutional coalitions in Italy made the choice of a republican form of government a compromised and negotiated solution rather than a dogmatic one, as had been the case in Spain.

Such compromise was also evident in the language employed in the new text—it was largely, if not entirely free of ideological content. The text was, however, sometimes ambiguous and of poor guideline quality. Indeed, the constitution often contained contradictory provisions. As in the recent Spanish case, some of the territorial provisions favored regional self-government in the more economically viable regions thus creating a constitutionalized form of inequality. Overall, the Italian constitutional political formula was the product of shifting but broadly representative coalitions where pragmatic (even if ambiguous) solutions helped to pave the way for the viable (even if imperfect) functioning of government (see Table 7.3).[12]

Germany. In Germany, the constitution-makers' foremost goal was to create a stable form of democracy where power could not be concentrated in the hands of one governmental branch or individual. United in this goal, the constitution-makers displayed little ideological behavior and a strong resolve to build an airtight form of democracy. They built upon the lessons learned from the breakdown of Weimar democracy incorporating provisions in the Basic Law that would counteract some of the abuses of that period.

Table 7.4 Outline of the German Federal Republic's Basic Law of 1949

I.	Basic Rights
II.	The Federation & the Lander
III.	The Bundestag
IV.	The Bundesrat
V.	The Federal President
VI.	The Federal Government
VII.	The Legislation of the Federation
VIII.	The Execution of Federal Laws & the Federal Administration
IX.	The Administration of Justice
X.	Finance
XI.	Transitory & Concluding Provisions

Source: Peter H. Merkl, The Origin of the West German Republic (New York: Oxford University Press, 1963), pp. 213-48.

The constitution-makers staged a two-pronged attack on such past abuses by creating a strong federal system and an accountable, but not powerless, prime minister (or chancellor). Paying particular attention to the relationship between the presidential office and the legislature, the constitution-makers decided to make that office largely ceremonial, devoid of extraordinary powers (such as the decree powers of the Weimar presidents). The chancellor could no longer be dismissed and appointed at the president's will but would owe his political survival to the new legislature (or Bundestag). One of the constitution-makers' cornerstones of regime stability was the constructive vote of no confidence. This type of vote (which the Spanish constitution-makers of 1977–78 adopted) assures some continuity during turbulent times by requiring the legislature to nominate a candidate for chancellor before rendering the extant chancellor powerless. In the German Basic Law of 1949 one finds not only maximum political compromise among the constitution-makers but also a clarity, pragmatism and resolution in its language which few constitutions surpass (see Table 7.4).[13]

Portugal. In the unamended Portuguese Constitution of 1976 one finds a political formula very much colored by the socio-political events of the time. Throughout this formula is an acknowledgment of the political role of the military, which, in many ways, had made the turning point toward democratization possible. Constitutionalizing the republican form of government, the political formula provided for a prime minister who would hold effective power. The constitution entrusted the prime minister with the task of guiding the nation towards a socialist economic system. The document also provided the system with a president. Elected by universal suffrage, the president had dual responsibilities—as President of the Council of the Revolution and as Supreme Commander of the Armed Forces. The Council of the Revolution, an advisory body with powers beyond merely advisory ones, would closely supervise the president, however, especially in giving him its assent to dissolve parliament. This Council was composed of

> the Chief and Deputy Chief of Staff, the three service chiefs, the Premier (if a military man) and fourteen officers (eight chosen by the army, three each by the navy and air force).[14]

The Council would in addition

> guarantee the functioning of democracy and the Constitution in line with 'the spirit of April 25,' and be the political and legislative organ in military matters.[15]

These constitutional solutions were largely the result of unilateral decision-making by the predominant leftist coalition, heavily influenced by the Armed Forces Movement. The language often had dogmatic overtones. Due to its excessive length, frequent ambiguity and the unresolved nature of some issues, the constitution was, as well, not easily implementable. Finally, there was a special proviso that no constitutional revisions could be made until 1980, leaving constitutional control in the interim, for all intents and purposes, in the military's hands (see Table 7.5).[16]

The Sociogovernmental Formula in Comparative Perspective

As seen in Chapter 6, the Spanish sociogovernmental formula presented a mixed picture. Issues involving the rights and freedoms of individuals were relatively broadly agreed upon and clearly spelled out. Unilateral conservative decision-making sometimes succeeded concerning certain "morality" issues. In most cases, however, these issues (namely abortion, divorce and education) were resolved multilaterally, though sometimes at the expense of clarity. The powers of the state during emergencies were set forth somewhat ambiguously as well, leaving a potentially dangerous lacuna in the protection of individual rights. Although it was effectively depoliticized, the role of the military was (diplomatically) treated with respect. Ambiguity resulted from the constitution-makers'

Table 7.5 Outline of the Portuguese Constitution of 1976

Preamble
I.   Fundamental Rights & Duties
II.   Economic Organization
III. Organization of Political Power
      1. General Principles
      2. President of the Republic
      3. Council of the Revolution
      4. Assembly of the Republic
      5. Government
      6. Courts
      7. Autonomous Regions
      8. Local Government
      9. Public Administration
     10. Armed Forces
IV.   Safeguards and Revisions of the
      Constitution
V.   Final & Transitory Provisions

Source: Constitution of the Portuguese Republic (Lisbon: Office of the Secretary of State for Mass Communications, Directorate General for Information and Diffusion, 1977).

struggle to remain consensual on the issue of church-state relations. While largely undogmatic in character, the Spanish sociogovernmental formula also left several issues unresolved, giving the new regime the weighty task of tackling such potentially explosive matters.

Spain 1931. The Spanish sociogovernmental formula of 1931 proved disastrous in its consequences because of the constitution-makers' unilateral decision-making and lack of political tact in constitutionalizing dogmatic solutions to church-state relations, the military and labor matters. The dangers of such confrontational decision-making should have been obvious at a time of such profound national crises. It is clear today, however, that constitution-makers contemplating such a course of action during a transition to democracy should beware of confrontational tactics and dogmatic solutions as it may prove self-destructive in the long run (see Table 7.2).[17]

Italy. For the most part, the Italian constitution-makers carefully and multilaterally decided sociogovernmental issues. Church and state were clearly separated in Article 7. Yet, unlike the earlier Spanish case, no deep polarization between clerical and anti-clerical forces existed in Italy. The absence of such polarization made the decision of separating church and state largely uneventful. The Italian constitution-makers, unlike the constitution-makers of the Spanish Second Republic, had obviously done their homework in examining whether such a decision would have an adverse impact on the nation. The military was placed in a secondary position similar to that of the civil service in Article 98. Individual liberties were comprehensively spelled out in Articles 13 through 54. Thus, the sociogovernmental formula of the Italian Constitution of 1947 displayed features that neither exacerbated extant problems nor created new ones. Where it did tackle issues, it did so in a relatively clear and straightforward manner (see Table 7.3).[18]

Germany. In Germany, effective compromise among the constitution-makers on sociogovernmental issues resulted in clear, guideline language. Learning lessons from both the Weimar and Nazi disasters, the constitution-makers were very careful to carve out, on the one hand, guarantees of fundamental democratic freedoms and, on the other hand, limitations on potentially arbitrary and excessive state power. If the constitution-makers erred in one of these areas it would be in that of granting the state more than enough police power. The document, however, remains an example of constitutional clarity and compromise (see Table 7.4).[19]

Portugal. An overly lengthy treatment of sociogovernmental issues characterizes the Portuguese Constitution. At times, these issues are handled dogmatically as in the case of agrarian reform, to which a whole section of the constitution is dedicated. Article 96, for instance, begins with the statement "Agrarian reform is one of the fundamental institutions for the building of socialist society . . ."[20] Some of the sociogovernmental formula language also displays ambiguity giving it an often unimplementable or rhetorical quality (see Table 7.5).[21]

Comparative Constitutional Formulas

Sociogovernmental formulas seem to be more frequently vague and ambiguous than political formulas. This seems to be the case in Italy, contemporary Spain and Portugal. Clarity is not impossible, however, as the German case and parts of each of the other constitutions prove. What is perhaps more significant vis-a-vis the viability of the new regime is whether either or both formulas contain dogmatic language. Where dogmatic constitutional language exists, the potential for destabilizing the government and/or exacerbating sociopolitical divisions is greater. The case of the Spanish Second Republic illustrates this point dramatically. So does Portugal in its treatment of landlord-peasant relations. Likewise, political or sociogovernmental issues that are only partially resolved in the constitution (or not resolved at all) will continue to be sources of political conflict in the post-constitutional period.

Table 7.6 Comparative Constitution-making Processes and Outcomes

Case Study	Preceding Regime	Major Factors Facilitating Transition	Predominant Party & Coalition	Constitution-Making Process* & Duration	Constitutional Outcome*
Spain (1931)	Authoritarian: Primo de Rivera 1923-1931	-Regime Breakdown -Pluralization -Military Non-Intervention	-Socialist Party -Leftist Coalition	-Actively Dissensual -6 Months	Dogmatic Guideline Constitution
Italy	Authoritarian: Mussolini 1922-1945	-Military Defeat -External Democratic Pressure -Pluralization	-Center-Right Party -Multilateral Coalition	-Consensual -7 Months	Compromise Ambiguous Constitution
Germany	Totalitarian: Hitler 1933-1945	-Military Defeat -External Imposition of Democracy -Capable Domestic Elite	-Center-Right Party -Multilateral Coalition	-Consensual -9 1/2 Months	Compromise Guideline Constitution
Portugal	Authoritarian: Salazar & Caetano 1932-1974	-Regime Breakdown -Military Coup -Pluralization	-Socialist Party -Leftist Coalition	-Passively Dissensual -11 1/2 Months	Dogmatic Ambiguous Constitution
Contemporary Spain	Authoritarian: Franco 1939-1975	-Pluralization -Elite Auto-Ruptura	-Center-Right Party -Multilateral Coalition	-Consensual -18 Months	Compromise Ambiguous Constitution

Note: *See Chapter 8 for elaborations on the concepts used in these two columns.

From this brief survey of political and sociogovernmental formulas, several preliminary observations about the constitution-making process can be made. Table 7.6 summarizes several of these findings. Only in Germany is there the best of both worlds—a pragmatic constitution with guideline value. Such a coincidence may be largely due to the constitution-makers' restrained coalitional behavior and the predominance of multilateral decision-making. In other cases—namely Italy and contemporary Spain—non-dogmatic constitutions that have mixed practical qualities seem to have emerged out of largely consensual processes. Thus a link seems to exist between a consensual process and a moderately implementable constitution. There appears to be another relationship between dissensual constitution-making and dogmatic solutions. Witness the cases of the Spanish Second Republic, where such dogmatic language was clearly implementable and Portugal, where the ambiguity of much of such language may have been in the long run a blessing in disguise.

Notes

1. See generally, Stanley Payne, *A History of Spain and Portugal*, Volume II (Madison, Wisconsin: University of Wisconsin Press, 1973); special issue of *Revista de Derecho Politico*, No. 12, entitled "La Constitucion de 1931 y el regimen politico de la II Republica" (Madrid, winter 1981–82); and, Juan J. Linz, "From Great Hopes to Civil War: The Breakdown of Democracy in Spain," in *The Breakdown of Democratic Regimes: Europe*, eds., Juan J. Linz and Alfred Stepan (Baltimore, Maryland: The Johns Hopkins Press, 1978).

2. See generally, John Clarke Adams and Paolo Barile, *The Government of Republican Italy* (Boston: Houghton Mifflin Co., 1972); and, Raphael Zariski, *Italy: The Politics of Uneven Development* (Hinsdale, Illinois: The Dryden Press, Inc., 1972).

3. See generally, Jorge Braga de Macedo and Simon Serfaty, eds., *Portugal Since the Revolution: Economic and Political Perspectives* (Boulder, Colorado: Westview Press, 1981); Rona M. Fields, *The Portuguese Revolution and the Armed Forces Movement* (New York, New York: Praeger Publishers, 1976); Juan J. Linz, "Europe's Southern Frontier: Evolving Trends Towards What?," *Daedalus* (1979); and, R. A. H. Robinson, *Contemporary Portugal* (London: George Allen and Unwin, Ltd.), pp. 167–275.

4. See generally, Karl Dietrich Bracher, *The German Dictatorship* (New York: Praeger Publishers, 1970); Peter Gay, *Weimar Culture* (New York: Harper & Row, 1968); and, Rainer Lepsius, "From Fragmented Party Democracy to Government by Emergency Decree," in *The Breakdown of Democratic Regimes: Europe*, eds., Linz and Stepan, pp. 34–79.

5. See references in note 4, especially Bracher, pp. 191–98 and Lepsius.

6. See references in note 1, especially *Revista de Estudios Politicos*.

7. See references in note 2.

8. One of the few works dealing almost exclusively with the role of a constitution in the emergence of a new democracy is the following study of the birth of the German Federal Republic: Peter H. Merkl, *The Origin of the West German Republic* (New York, New York: Oxford University Press, 1963).

9. *Constitution of the Portuguese Republic* (Lisbon: Office of the Secretary of State for Mass Communications, Directorate General for Information and Diffusion, 1976), p. 16A.

10. See Fields, *The Portuguese Revolution and the Armed Forces Movement.*

11. See Linz, "From Great Hopes to Civil War . . ."

12. See references in note 2, especially Adams and Barile, *The Government of Republican Italy* and, *Constitution of the Republic of Italy* (Rome: Chamber of Deputies, Senate of the Republic, 1979), especially pp. 42–48.

13. See Merkl, *The Origin of the West German Republic.* See especially the entire Basic Law reprinted in Merkl's Appendix II, pp. 213–48.

14. Robinson, *Contemporary Portugal,* p. 258. Also see, *Constitution of the Portuguese Republic,* especially articles 111–149.

15. Robinson, *Contemporary Portugal,* pp. 257–60.

16. Robinson, *Contemporary Portugal,* pp. 257–60.

17. See references in note 1.

18. See references in note 12, especially, *Constitution of the Republic of Italy,* pp. 12, 15–20 and 37.

19. See reference in note 13.

20. *Constitution of the Portuguese Republic,* p. 59. Also see articles 12–110, pp. 21–65.

21. *Constitution of the Portuguese Republic,* p. 59. Also see references in note 3.

8

A Theory of Transitions from Authoritarianism to Democracy: The Centrality of the Constitution-making Process

Introduction

This chapter weaves together the various findings of this work to provide a theoretical framework for understanding transitions to democracy. The framework is based on this study's argument that the constitution-making process is central to a successful transition to democracy. Its significance is based both on the evolution of the process qua process and the content of the constitutional outcome.

The framework consists of several parts each of which addresses a major developmental aspect of the transition. When are potential turning points towards democratization possible? Once a turning point takes place, what must follow before a viable constitution-making process can begin? What types of constitution-making processes and outcomes are possible and what is their interrelationship? How does the sociopolitical climate of the nation affect the process and how does it, in turn, affect the climate? Does the type of transition that takes place have any relation to the type of democracy that eventually emerges?

The Turning Point Toward Democratization

Two major developments must coincide to create the proper conditions for a successful turning point—authoritarian decline and sociopolitical pluralization. On the one hand, the authoritarian regime must be experiencing some type of internal or external crisis. An internal crisis can take various forms. The death or deposition of the existing leader(s) may occasion a leadership crisis. Such a crisis may also take place as a result of intra-authoritarian elite rivalry. The authoritarian regime's ineffective institutional framework or policy mismanagement may bring about an institutional or policy crisis. The elite's inability to cope with any one of a number of social, economic or political problems, including rapid economic modernization, sociopolitical pluralization or regional/ ethnic dissatisfaction could bring about such a crisis. By choosing to liberalize, the authoritarian elite itself may cause a third type of internal crisis affecting its viability—a liberalization crisis. The principal external cause of authoritarian decline would be that of an unsuccessful foreign military crisis. The economic and moral humiliation of military defeat can either destroy the leadership or render it governmentally ineffective.

The other key ingredient for the success of a potential turning point is sociopolitical pluralization. As described in Chapter 1, sociopolitical pluralization can take one of two forms—organized long-term pluralization or spontaneous, shorter-term pluralization. Either form, at the right time, can aid in the successful resolution of a turning point. Obviously, long-term pluralization can be more effective as it is well organized and continuous. Such pluralization exerts a greater pressure on the authoritarian regime and is in a better position to take advantage of any of the aforementioned regime crises. Whether long-term or short-term, pluralization during a regime crisis may not be sufficient to produce a successful turning point. A key, although not absolutely necessary, component of either type of pluralization is the existence of a nationally recognizable and charismatic opposition leader. For a turning point to be successful without such a visible contender will be more difficult, although not impossible. In such situations where the opposition is divided or lacks unified leadership, the authoritarian regime is in a far better position to maintain control. Based on the various forms authoritarian decline and sociopolitical pluralization can take and their potential coincidence in time, it is possible to identify several types of turning points.

The Ruptura Turning Point

A ruptura turning point is one in which, on the crest of sociopolitical pluralization, an opposition elite replaces the authoritarian elite and makes a relatively rapid and clean break with the past. This type of turning point is likely to occur when either form of pluralization is present and an unpredictable or abrupt authoritarian crisis (the death of the leader, military defeat) takes place. A wholly new and previously excluded elite fills the political vacuum. Such a dramatic turning point is somewhat dangerous, however. A potentially anarchical political situation may emerge in which quick decisions are made but larger issues are ignored. Spain in the 1930s and Portugal in the 1970s provide examples of ruptura turning points (see Table 8.1).

Table 8.1 Types of Turning Points Toward Democratization

	Principal Factors in Authoritarian Regime Decline		
The Level of Sociopolitical Pluralization	Governmental/ Institutional Breakdown	Military Defeat Abroad	Authoritarian Elite Chooses to liberalize
Extensive Pluralization	RUPTURA	RUPTURA	AUTO-RUPTURA
Moderate Pluralization	RUPTURA or REFORM	RUPTURA or REFORM	REFORM or AUTO-RUPTURA
Minimal or No Pluralization	CONTINUITY	REFORM	REFORM

Note: These designations are approximations. Ruptura could, e.g., take place in a nation without much pluralization or not subject to external military or political pressures. It is, however, likely that a given turning point will result from the prevalence of the relevant two conditions illustrated in this Table.

The Reform Turning Point

A reform turning point occurs when, in the face of growing socio-political pluralization, the authoritarian elite chooses gradual liberal-ization. Such liberalization begins with reform without regime change. Regime change may be on the distant horizon of the elite's agenda and may be (and is) repeatedly postponed. It is possible, however, for actual democratization to evolve out of such a path. None of the transitions reviewed here started with a reform turning point. The beginning of the long Brazilian transition to democracy (from the late 1970s through the mid-1980s) is a good example of such a turning point.

The Auto-ruptura Turning Point

An auto-ruptura turning point may occur when the authoritarian elite causes a liberalization crisis by choosing to break with the past as a response to long-term pluralization. This turning point differs from the reform turning point in that the elite breaks with authoritarian practices and begins democratization immediately. The policy of reform with regime change is on the immediate agenda—not as something to be attained in the distant future. The auto-ruptura turning point also differs from that of reform because of its more developed sociopolitical plur-alization. This type of turning point is less risky than the ruptura variety but more effective than the sluggish reform turning point. Spain in the 1970s may become the classic example of auto-ruptura (see Table 8.1).

The External Defeat Turning Point

The authoritarian elite's inept handling of a military crisis may bring about an external defeat turning point. The victorious forces (which must be democratic) actually impose or demand the creation of democracy in the defeated nation. This may be the only type of turning point where the presence of either form of pluralization is not absolutely necessary. Any pluralization will, of course, be helpful to the building of democracy, and a small core of domestic democratic leaders must exist to carry out such democratization. But, as the case of Germany showed, the existence of either type of pluralization at the turning point is not essential as long as it eventually develops to sustain the emerging democracy.

Italy exhibits this type of turning point as well. Unlike Germany, in Italy there was pluralization, however. This difference explains in part why, in Italy, the allies only demanded the creation of democracy while, in the case of Germany, they actively supervised the imposition of democracy. Barring unforeseeable international circumstances, it is difficult to envision today too many cases of external defeat turning points (see Table 8.1).

The Turning Point Analysis

This analysis has two uses. On the one hand, an examination of the internal and external crises of a current authoritarian regime together with its level of pluralization can yield a forecast of probable, possible and unlikely scenarios. Such an analysis can be of substantial value to both domestic and external policy-makers.

On the other hand, the application of this analysis to an ongoing or recent turning point may help the observer to discern the type of transition that is unfolding. Following the more abrupt ruptura turning point, the chances of a riskier and quicker transition are greater. The possibility of a delayed democratization is, however, greatest in the case of a reform turning point. A more balanced and consensual transition may result from auto-ruptura as the authoritarian elite disarms its most vehement opposition by breaking with past practices while simultaneously opening up political participation. Finally, democratization resulting from the external defeat turning point is potentially elitist. Such elitism results from the lower level (or non-existence) of pluralization in the defeated nation. Only in the more distant future may the true hold of democracy in that nation become evident.

The Pre-Constitutional Period

Important to the success of the transition is the degree of democratization that takes place in the pre-constitutional period—after the turning point and prior to the constitution-making process. Is such reform limited to socioeconomic matters or does it address broader sociopolitical problems? How far do the political reforms go? What freedoms and rights are being granted to individuals and what limits or constraints are being placed on authoritarian structures and/or practices? The comprehensive or limited character of pre-constitutional reform may have an impact on the constitution-making process. A limited set of reforms may make that process more tedious and problematic. It may also make that process potentially less legitimate and its results less acceptable to society.

Comprehensive Pre-Constitutional Reform

This type of reform occurs when the transitionary elite implements political and sociogovernmental reforms necessary for the proper preliminary democratic functioning of the nation. Such proper functioning can only take place if there is some legal basis and certainty that fundamental human rights will be respected, political participation will be uninhibited and sufficiently free preparations are possible for nationwide pre-constitutional elections. The following conditions must therefore be developing:

1. A process of sociopolitical legalization in which authoritarian controls on basic freedoms are lifted and secured by a temporary, pre-constitutional law or decree. Such basic freedoms would minimally include freedom of speech, of the press, of association and of freedom from arbitrary or political encarceration.
2. A process of authoritarian illegalization in which, at a minimum, constraints and prohibitions are placed on the most arbitrary authoritarian devices, namely the police (and the military) and other flagrantly authoritarian institutions.
3. The democratization of essential pre-constitutional practices including the legalization of political parties, the drafting of a temporary (and fair) electoral law, the initiation and conduct of an open political campaign and the holding of nationwide legislative elections.

Limited Pre-Constitutional Reform

Limited pre-constitutional reform occurs whenever one of these major elements is missing from a pre-constitutional period. Depending on the nature of the missing element(s), implications for the viability of the transition generally may follow. If, for instance, political parties cannot assemble legally or the press cannot print uncensored stories or individuals cannot speak without retribution, then the process of democratization is at best tentative and at worst jeopardized.

Among the cases examined here, Germany is the best example of limited pre-constitutional reform, as no nationwide elections preceded its constitution-making process. Notwithstanding such limitations, however, the German transition was among the smoothest and least problematic of the five cases examined. Of course, the unique historical realities of the German case need not be reiterated.

The Analysis of Pre-Constitutional Reform

An examination of the comprehensive or limited nature of a nation's pre-constitutional period provides an additional clue about the continuing viability of the transition. Where there is a fairly comprehensive pre-constitutional reform—including sociopolitical legalization, authoritarian illegalization and the democratization of essential pre-constitutional practices—the chances of a legitimate process and transition are greater.

Where, on the other hand, there is limited pre-constitutional reform, the legitimacy (both real and perceived) of the constitution-making process and the transition may be imperiled. If, for example, certain political parties are not legalized (thereby excluding them from pre-constitutional elections) or certain authoritarian practices are continued (such as politically motivated arrests), the success of the process and of the transition may be severely jeopardized. As a consequence of these actions, those excluded from politics or those affected by arbitrary power (and social sectors backing them) may no longer support the waning democratic character of the transition. The objective reality (and societal perception) of such legitimacy is an important ingredient in the continuing viability of the transition. Without such legitimacy, opposition to the transitionary elite's policies (concerning both the constitution and other matters) will grow and so will the conditions for another (perhaps more violent) type of political change.

The Constitution-making Process and Outcome

The constitution-making process is the core of the transition. While the turning point signals the beginning of the transition, and pre-constitutional reforms lay down the necessary groundwork, an effective constitution-making process creates the legal framework for regime change and comprehensive democratization.

The Process

The analysis of the constitution-making process consists of an examination of coalitional strategies and of negotiating techniques. In most cases, the results of the pre-constitutional elections will determine the composition of the constituent body. The potential coalitional strategy of each party can be projected from its share of the vote. Ideological compatibility among some of the relevant parties can be a critical factor in those parties' strategic coalitional thinking. Central to this analysis is determining whether a party on either end of the political spectrum (left or right) has received a (parliamentary) majority or whether such a party can attain a majority by coalescing with another party(ies) of similar ideological persuasion. In either one of these cases, there is a potential for ideologically unilateral (and potentially polarized) coalitions. Other factors, such as the relative pragmatism (governmental orientation) of a party and its leader(s), influence such coalitional strategies, however.

The preceding turning point and type of pre-constitutional reform may also have an impact on the course of events.

The second prong of this analysis consists of an assessment of negotiating techniques between the parties and/or coalitions. Confrontational negotiations are more likely to result from the predominance of an ideological coalition that attempts to impose unilateral constitutional decision-making. If the excluded parties are ideologically compatible they may, in turn, form a (potentially effective) minority coalition, creating a dangerously polarized situation. Where such excluded parties are incompatible, they might independently (although ineffectually) oppose the predominant coalition. The only possible benefit of such unilateralism is that decision-making will be rapid and may yield clear constitutional results. When the predominant coalition is multilateral, however, there is a greater likelihood of accommodation. Concomitant to such accommodation, in turn, is the possibility of greater ambiguity in the resulting constitutional language.

The examination of the coalitional strategies and negotiating techniques of a process through its political phases provides a roadmap of that process. Representing the major steps through which the process unwinds, the phases reflect changes in coalitional strategies (from unilateral to multilateral or vice-versa) and/or negotiating techniques (from accommodation to confrontation or the reverse). This political phase analysis can yield useful lessons because from it general observations can be made about the ideological or pragmatic, unilateral or multilateral and confrontational or accommodational character of the process. One may discern from these findings the overall consensual or dissensual character not only of the process but also of the transition and the emerging democracy.

Based on the analysis of the Spanish case along these lines and the review of the four mini-case studies, it is possible to formulate a typology of constitution-making processes. This typology distinguishes four main types of process—the consensual, passively dissensual, actively dissensual and the stillborn (see Table 8.2).

The Consensual Process. The predominant coalition in a consensual process is multilateral and non-ideological and the prevailing form of negotiation is one of accommodation. Among the cases examined earlier, post-war Germany and Italy and contemporary Spain display this type of process.

In Germany, consensus was a result of both external pressure and internal political realities. The possibility of unilateral opposing coalitions and confrontation was, however, real—with the CDU/CSU forming a conservative camp with the FDP and the SPD creating a leftist coalition with the KPD (see Table 7.1). The German constitution-making process

Table 8.2 Typology of Constitution-making Processes during
Transitions to Democracy

		Coalitional Strategies of Constitution-makers	
		Non-Ideological & Multilateral	Ideological & Unilateral
Mode			
of	Accommodation	Consensual (Germany, Italy & Spain 1970s)	Passively Dissensual (Portugal)
Nego-			
tia-			
tion	Confrontation	Actively Dissensual	Actively Dissensual or Stillborn (Spain 1930s)

instead exhibited coalitional flexibility, multilateralism and the prevalence of a consensual coalition between the CDU/CSU, SPD and FDP.

In Italy there was an even greater potential for a predominant ideological coalition—between the communists and the socialists—as they, together with sympathetic smaller leftist parties, could have easily commanded a parliamentary majority (see Table 7.1). Instead, accommodation and fluctuating coalitions prevailed.

Finally, Spain also exhibited the necessary conditions for a polarized constitution-making process. While the election winner—the UCD—did not have a parliamentary majority, it could have fashioned a predominant conservative coalition with the strongest right-wing party—the AP. Likewise, the second largest party—the PSOE—could have mustered a substantial leftist coalition with the PCE, regional parties and other left-leaning parliamentary groups. While the UCD and AP formed an intermittent winning coalition on specific issues, such a coalition was in no way comprehensive or predominant. Instead of displaying polarization, the Spanish process may be a model of consensual politics—where parties of widely differing ideologies, through accommodation, formed the predominant multilateral (consensual) coalition.

The Passively Dissensual Process. The passively dissensual process is one in which the predominant coalition is ideological and decision-making is unilateral but largely non-confrontational. The absence of confrontation is due either to the fact that the constitution-makers are not imposing dogmatic solutions or to the disorganization of the remaining parties. Their passivity or inability to agree renders these parties incapable of creating an effective opposing (perhaps ideological) coalition. Contemporary Portugal comes closest to exemplifying this type of constitution-making process.

The Actively Dissensual Process. Confrontation and disagreement are synonymous with the actively dissensual process. It is not a process in which there needs to be a predominant ideological coalition. Based on the presence or absence of ideological coalitions, there are, however, two variants of this process. On the one hand, where ideological coalitions exist (and one of them is predominant), effective unilateral decision-making in a confrontational setting will probably prevail yielding a dogmatic constitution. An example of a process in which a predominant ideological coalition made unilateral constitutional decisions in a confrontational atmosphere is that of Spain in 1931.

There can also be, on the other hand, an actively dissensual process where there are no ideologically inspired opposing coalitions. Such a process would take place in an environment of political irresponsibility and severe inter-party disagreement and fragmentation (where coalitions are politically impossible). None of the cases reviewed in this book exhibit this variant of the actively dissensual process. It nevertheless remains a possible type of process in a post-authoritarian nation exhibiting poor party development, factionalism and personality-based politics.

The Stillborn Process. Finally, the stillborn process is, in a way, an unsuccessful variant of the actively dissensual process as it does not yield a constitution or yields one that is neither accepted nor implemented. Riddled with intensely confrontational negotiations, it is a process that irreversibly breaks down. The stillborn process may result from an ideologically coalitional setting where no one coalition is able to predominate. Such a process may also occur in a non-ideological setting where there is no majority party or coalition, and inter-party disagreement is such that it is impossible to form a predominant coalition. The central characteristic of the stillborn process is that a constitution is either not produced or, if it is drafted, is not nationally accepted. France in 1945–46 provides an example of this type of process.[1]

The Outcome

Useful lessons about a nation's political system can be learned from a content analysis of its constitution. The examination of the fundamental text resulting from a constitution-making process differs substantially, however, from typical constitutional analysis based on judicial interpretation. The analysis here focuses on whether the political and sociogovernmental formulas of the new text are largely dogmatic or pragmatic in content and whether they provide a clear or ambiguous guideline for future political action.

This content analysis, however, does not encompass the entire constitutional text. Each of the constitutional formulas consist of several major components. The analysis only focuses on these provisions:

1. The Political Formula:
   a. The definition of the new democratic regime
   b. The definition and description of democratic institutions
      (1) The functional balance of power:
         (a) The executive
         (b) The legislative
         (c) The judiciary
         (d) Other institutional bodies (e.g. the monarchy)
         (e) Their interrelationship
      (2) The territorial balance of power:
         (a) The territorial units of the nation
         (b) Their interrelationship.
2. The Sociogovernmental Formula:
   a. The relationship between the state and the individual
      (1) Rights and duties of the individual
      (2) Rights and duties of the state
      (3) Under "normal" and under "extraordinary" conditions
      (4) The military/police establishment
   b. The relationship between the state and major social sectors (e.g., church-state relations)

The major questions that need to be asked concerning the various components of each formula are the following:

1. What was the ideological behavior of each of the constitution-makers in resolving each of these issues—if they initially presented dogmatic positions, by the end of the process, did their views remain unchanged or become more pragmatic and consensual?
2. Can the content of a particular constitutional issue be characterized as largely dogmatic (i.e., representing the views of one ideological alternative) or compromised (i.e., representing an agreement among divergent views)?
3. Finally, does the language provide a clear guideline for implementation or is it largely ambiguous or rhetorical (and therefore unimplementable)?

Table 8.3   A Typology of Constitutional Outcomes during Transitions
            to Democracy

		Ideological Character of the Political & Sociogovernmental Formulas	
		Dogmatic	Compromise
Implement- ability of Key Cons-	Guideline Language	Dogmatic Guideline Constitution (Spain 1931)	Compromise Guideline Constitution (Germany)
titutional Provisions	Ambiguous Language	Dogmatic Ambiguous Constitution (Portugal)	Compromise Ambiguous Constitution (Italy & Spain 1978)

Based on this content analysis, it is possible to formulate a typology of constitutions resulting from constitution-making processes during transitions to democracy (see Table 8.3).

The Dogmatic Guideline Constitution. A dogmatic guideline constitution is one in which ideological language is evident in key parts of both formulas and clear directions make it largely implementable. A possible consequence of the implementation of a dogmatic constitution is that opposition to both the constitution and possibly the regime may exist among those excluded from effective participation in the constitution-making process. The Spanish Constitution of 1931 is an example of such a document and of such consequences.

The Dogmatic Ambiguous Constitution. A dogmatic ambiguous constitution displays ideological language in key parts of its formulas but is largely rhetorical or ambiguous in its political instructions. Social segments opposed to the constitutional solutions may try to amend or revise it. The ambiguity will limit the state's capacity to implement institutional/political changes. This limitation may, however, be a blessing in disguise as the new regime is incapable of implementing some of the dogmatic solutions that such social segments oppose. The unamended Portuguese Constitution of 1976 is an example of a dogmatic ambiguous constitution.

The Compromise Guideline Constitution. A compromise guideline constitution contains both consensual decisions and clear guideline language. Such compromise and straightforwardness will allow the state to implement institutional and political changes without major socio-political opposition. The coincidence of both compromise and clarity, however, is a rarity. The German Basic Law of 1949 is one of a few such examples.

The Compromise Ambiguous Constitution. This type of constitution has consensually agreed upon formulas but, as one of the side-effects of compromise, its language is often ambiguous. Such lack of clarity in key provisions renders the compromise ambiguous constitution only partially implementable. While there will be no major opposition to the constitution, attempts at reforming and amending its ambiguous parts will be likely. Both the Spanish Constitution of 1978 and the Italian Constitution have exhibited such problems, especially concerning their respective territorial/regional provisions.

The Relationship Between Constitution-making Process and Outcome

The next step in this analysis is to discover whether any relationships exist between the various types of process and outcome that have been distinguished. Based on the five case studies examined in this book, it is possible to differentiate two such interrelationships. As Table 8.4 suggests, however, there may be other possible patterns.

The Consensual/Compromise Pattern

The consensual/compromise pattern exists when a consensual process yields either a compromise guideline or compromise ambiguous constitution. Post-war Germany is an example of the former and Italy and contemporary Spain are examples of the latter interrelationship. In both variations of the pattern, there seems to be a nexus between accommodational/multilateral negotiations and a non-dogmatic constitution, whether or not it is clearly or ambiguously written.

The Dissensual/Dogmatic Pattern

The Portuguese case illustrates the interrelationship between a passively dissensual process and a dogmatic ambiguous constitution. A similar connection exists between the actively dissensual process and a dogmatic guideline constitution, as the Spanish case of 1931 confirms. These examples show that there is a link between an ideologically negotiated process and a dogmatic constitutional result (whether or not it is clearly or ambiguously written).

Table 8.4 The Relationship Between the Process and the Outcome: Constitutional Patterns

| | | Type of Constitution-Making Process | | |
| | | Consensual | Dissensual | |
			Passively	Actively
Type of Constitutional Outcome	Compromise Guideline Constitution	The Consensual/Compromise Pattern (Germany)	No Relationship Found (Possible)	No Relationship Found (Unlikely)
	Compromise Ambiguous Constitution	The Consensual/Compromise Pattern (Italy & Spain '78)	No Relationship Found (Possible)	No Relationship Found (Possible)
	Dogmatic Guideline Constitution	No Relationship Found (Unlikely)	No Relationship Found (Possible)	The Dissensual/Dogmatic Pattern (Spain '31)
	Dogmatic Ambiguous Constitution	No Relationship Found (Unlikely)	The Dissensual/Dogmatic Pattern (Portugal)	No Relationship Found (Possible)

Note: This Table only shows findings concerning the five cases examined in this Chapter. The comments "possible" and "unlikely" are suggestions of what other interrelationships might exist between a given constitution-making process and outcome.

Constitution-making Patterns and the Post-Constitutional Period

What seems to be crucial about these patterns is the relationship between the ideological or non-ideological character of the process, on the one hand, and the (respectively) dogmatic or non-dogmatic content of the resulting constitution, on the other. The guideline or ambiguous quality of the constitutional language does not seem to be a major factor in these relationships. What is important about the quality of the language, however, is whether or not the provisions of the constitution will be implementable in the post-constitution-making period.

The Predictability of Constitution-making Patterns. The electoral results of a pre-constitutional period will heavily influence the composition of the constituent body. The potential coalitional strategies emerging out of such electoral and constituent results will already provide a clue about the entire constitution-making pattern. Where polarized ideological coalitions result, the chances of a dogmatic constitution are greatest (e.g., Spain 1931 and Portugal). When a centrist party wins a majority or is capable of fashioning a predominant consensual coalition, the odds of a compromise constitutional result are high (e.g., Germany). When the electoral results, however, allow either route—that of polarized coalitions or that of a predominant consensual coalition—the political pragmatism and responsibility of the constitution-making elite is the only barrier against a dissensual process which could eventually yield a dogmatic constitution (e.g., Italy and Spain in the 1970s).

The Impact of Constitutions on the Emerging Regimes. The guideline or ambiguous quality of the constitutional language does not seem to be a major factor in establishing the patterns mentioned earlier as both ambiguous and guideline constitutions have resulted from both consensual and dissensual processes (see Table 8.4). The importance of the quality of such language, however, has to do with its impact on the post-constitution-making period as the new regime attempts to implement the provisions of the constitution.

When the resulting document is largely dogmatic, the importance of whether or not it is implementable will depend on how politically polarized or socially heterogeneous the nation is (i.e., on its sociopolitical climate). In a divided society, the regime's ability to implement a dogmatic guideline constitution may in fact exacerbate these divisions (e.g., Spain in the 1930s.) In a relatively homogeneous society that has undergone a passively dissensual process, the implementation of such a dogmatic guideline constitution may not have adverse effects.

Concomitantly, the difficulty of implementing a dogmatic ambiguous constitution will render it generally harmless in a socially divided (or politically polarized) nation (e.g., Portugal). Likewise, the impact of such a constitution will be minor in a socially homogeneous (or centripetal) nation (although it is unlikely that a dogmatic constitutional result will occur under such homogeneous circumstances). Lobbying to reform the constitution may be the most obvious consequence of such ambiguity.

In situations yielding compromise constitutions, other consequences are possible. Societal divisions or polarization do not factor too heavily into the implementation of these types of constitution. Compromise among the diverse political parties supposedly eliminated ideological solutions from the constitution. There would therefore be little, if any, ground for organized opposition to the constitution. The main problem concerning the implementation of compromise constitutions, is that they are more likely to contain ambiguous or vague provisions because clarity is often a necessary sacrifice in attaining compromise. Obviously, these comments do not apply to the compromise guideline constitution which is the most desirable type of constitution that can possibly emerge out of a constitution-making process. The worst consequence, then, of a compromise ambiguous constitution is that important sections are unimplementable, certain aspects of democratization are potentially delayed and revisions of the constitution, a time-consuming and costly affair, must follow.

The Sociopolitical Climate of the Transition

Before the analyst, armed with conclusions about a turning point, preconstitutional period, and constitution-making pattern, goes on to assess the overall transition, he/she must take into account the sociopolitical climate of the nation at the time.

A clear picture of a particular nation's sociopolitical climate may be gleaned from two inquiries. First, what are the nation's major historical social divisions—are there significant religious cleavages or conflicts (e.g., Protestant/Catholic, clerical/anti-clerical); are there distinct ethnic groups, regions, linguistic and cultural segments of society and, if so, do they adhere to particular political groups?; are there deep economic or class divisions between such groups as a small landowning minority and a vast impoverished peasantry?

The second inquiry is whether political polarization exists or has the potential to emerge. Does a review of electoral and other sociological and historical data reveal the potential for ideological polarization on a left/right spectrum? Does this analysis indicate that a polarized party system (devoid of a viable center), a moderately polarized system (with strong extremes but a viable center), or a centripetal system (with a very strong center) exists or is developing?

For purposes of the characterizations that follow, a society is considered heterogeneous if it exhibits two or more major social divisions—of a religious, economic and/or ethnic/regional nature. A society is politically polarized when its electoral results yield politically relevant, ideologically distinct parties or coalitions on both ends of the political spectrum. Polarization is, in addition, greatest where the political center is not particularly strong or viable on its own. Table 8.5 summarizes the character of the sociopolitical climate in each of the five cases examined here:

1. In Spain in the 1930s social heterogeneity—evident in clerical/anti-clerical religious divisions and regional and economic disparities—together with a polarized political situation yielded what might be called a heterogeneous/polarized climate.
2. In Germany, on the other hand, minimal social differentiations and an almost total absence of political polarization resulted in a homogeneous/centripetal climate.
3. After World War Two, Italy had a north/south socioeconomic division which was to become more developed with time. No other major social divisions were evident. Although not actually practiced in the process, political polarization was, however, a distinct possibility (and later reality) making this a homogeneous/semi-polarized climate.
4. Portugal exhibited a climate similar to but more extreme than the Italian. While economic divisions were fairly deep, especially between landlords and peasants, no other major social divisions existed. Together with its developed political polarization, the Portuguese case was one with a homogeneous/polarized climate.
5. Finally, contemporary Spain is difficult to categorize. The electoral results yielded the possibility (but not the reality) of polarization. The political composition of Spain at the time could at best be characterized as semi-polarized. Such semi-polarization, together with distinct regional and economic (and some would contend, religious) divisions characterize Spain as a heterogeneous/semi-polarized climate.

The social homogeneity of a nation will aid the elite in implementing political change since the potential for intra-social conflict remains low. Social heterogeneity, however, can be a hindrance to easy or peaceful decision-making. Targeted social segments will be much more sensitive and quick to oppose any measures adversely affecting them. Political

Table 8.5 The Sociopolitical Background of Several Transitions to Democracy

		National Cases				
		Spain 1930s	Germany	Italy	Portugal	Spain 1970s
Social Divisions	Religious	Yes	No	No	No	No
	Ethnic/Linguistic	Yes	No	No	No	Yes
	Economic	Yes	No	Yes	Yes	Yes
Political Divisions	Ideological Polarization	Yes	No	Mixed	Yes	Mixed
The Overall Sociopolitical Picture		Heterogeneous & Polarized	Homogeneous & Centripetal	Homogeneous & Semi-Polarized	Homogeneous & Polarized	Heterogeneous & Semi-Polarized

Table 8.6   A Typology of Transitions from Authoritarian to
            Democratic Regimes

		The Sociopolitical Picture during the Transition	
		Homogeneous and Centripetal	Heterogeneous and/or Polarized
The	The Consensual/ Compromise	THE UNFETTERED TRANSITION	THE CONSENSUAL TRANSITION
Constitu-	Pattern	(Germany)	(Italy & Spain 1970s)
tional	The Dissensual/ Dogmatic	THE CONFRONTATIONAL TRANSITION	THE POLARIZED TRANSITION
Pattern	Pattern		(Spain 1930s & Portugal)

polarization within society will add an intense additional burden to the transitionary elite—with political unrest always a possibility. Reflecting such polarization within its own ranks, the elite thus has additional obstacles to overcome if it tries to pursue a consensual process. Political centripetality, on the other hand, will be a bonus for decision-makers as political threats from the extremes will be minimized and a consensual focus will be easier to come by.

The Transition to Democracy

Until now, it has not been possible to tackle the overall issue of what types of transition to democracy exist. Based on all the inquiries made up to this point, Table 8.6 provides a typology of transitions to democracy.

The Unfettered Transition

An unfettered transition is most likely to occur in a nation with a homogeneous/centripetal climate and the potential for a consensual/ compromise constitution-making pattern. Such a transition has a very good chance of proceeding smoothly—without major sociopolitical obstacles—and of yielding a broadly acceptable constitution and democracy. A clear example of an unfettered transition was that of Germany as it became the Federal Republic.

The Consensual Transition

This type of transition may take place in a nation where either or both social heterogeneity and political polarization are present and the consensual/compromise pattern is possible. Thus, nations with either a heterogeneous/polarized, heterogeneous/semi-polarized, heterogeneous/centripetal, or homogeneous/polarized climate may experience a consensual transition. The ingredient that allows any one of these settings to undergo a consensual (rather than a confrontational or polarized transition) is the politically pragmatic and responsible attitude of the elite, including the constitution-makers. Because of the heterogeneity and/or polarization, this type of transition is more difficult to implement smoothly than the unfettered transition. It is consensual, however, because of the elite's overriding pragmatic drive, especially during the constitution-making process, to practice the non-ideological politics of accommodation and multilateral decision-making. The postwar Italian and contemporary Spanish transitions to democracy provide examples of consensual transitions.

The Confrontational Transition

In this type of transition, a society that has a homogeneous/centripetal climate nevertheless experiences a dissensual/dogmatic constitution-making pattern. Although it is hard to visualize this type of transition without a case study to illustrate it, it is conceivable for such a transition to take place in a nation where intense (even though centripetal) elite rivalries overshadow the relatively quiet sociopolitical climate. The resulting constitution (whether dogmatic or compromised) is likely to be fairly ambiguous as a result of such continual confrontation.

The Polarized Transition

This is a transition in which either or both sociopolitical divisions and political polarization exist and the dissensual/dogmatic pattern is most likely. This transition is the potentially most volatile of the four types profiled. Within both the elite and society, divisions and/or polarization constantly threaten the continuing viability of the transition. The resulting dogmatic document is bound to perpetuate and potentially exacerbate these divisions and does not bode well for the long-term survival of the new regime. The Spanish Second Republic experienced such a transition with eventually ominous consequences. The recent Portuguese transition was also polarized but continues to exist.

A Summary of Transitions

Table 8.7 provides a summary overview of each of the steps through which the five transitions examined in this book developed. Several further observations can now be added to the ones already made:

- In the cases of Spain (1931) and Portugal, ruptura turning points were followed by dissensual/dogmatic patterns in polarized climates yielding overall polarized transitions.
- In postwar Italy and Germany, external defeat turning points were followed by consensual compromise patterns in somewhat different sociopolitical climates. Such differences may help to explain partly why Italy had an overall consensual transition and Germany an unfettered transition.
- Spain in the 1970s exhibits an auto-ruptura turning point, followed by a consensual compromise pattern in a heterogeneous/semi-polarized sociopolitical climate yielding an overall consensual transition.

It is not possible to determine conclusively whether these are transitionary patterns unique to the cases presented here. There is, however, a predictive value to the exposition of these patterns—while no two transitions are exactly alike, there seem to be certain recurring interrelationships:

1. Between a ruptura turning point, a heterogenous and/or polarized climate and a dissensual/dogmatic pattern (e.g., Spain (1931) and Portugal);
2. Between an external defeat turning point and the need to follow a consensual/compromise pattern from which either an unfettered or a consensual transition will emerge (e.g., Germany and Italy); and,
3. Between the authoritarian elite's decision to break with its own past through an auto-ruptura turning point in the face of a well developed heterogeneous and/or polarized climate, a consensual/compromise pattern and an overall consensual transition (e.g., contemporary Spain).

Beyond the Transition

Although many issues remain unexplored, there is one more question this book will address—does a relationship exist between the type of transition that evolves and the type of democracy that emerges? For

Table 8.7 A Summary of Transitionary Routes toward Democracy

Case	Turning Point	The Pre-Constitutional Period	The Constitutional Period			The Socio-Political Picture	Overall Type of Transition
			Process	Outcome	Pattern		
SPAIN (1930s)	Ruptura	Complete	Actively Dissensual	Dogmatic Guideline	Dissensual Dogmatic	Heterogeneous & Polarized	POLARIZED
GERMANY	External Defeat & Ruptura	Incomplete	Consensual	Compromise Guideline	Consensual Compromise	Homogeneous & Centripetal	UNFETTERED
ITALY	External Defeat & Ruptura	Complete	Consensual	Compromise Ambiguous	Consensual Compromise	Homogeneous & Semi-Polarized	CONSENSUAL
SPAIN (1970s)	Auto-ruptura	Complete	Consensual	Compromise Ambiguous	Consensual Compromise	Heterogeneous & Semi-Polarized	CONSENSUAL
PORTUGAL	Ruptura	Complete	Passively Dissensual	Dogmatic Ambiguous	Dissensual Dogmatic	Homogeneous & Polarized	POLARIZED

this purpose and based on certain findings in this book, it is necessary to construct a typology of democratic regimes that takes into account a form of elite behavior that has not frequently been distinguished—that of accommodational behavior.

A Typology of Democracies

Drawing heavily on Arend Lijphart's excellent typology of democratic regimes in *Democracy in Plural Societies*, it is possible to distinguish six types of democracy.[2] This typology (as does Lijphart's) consists of two major factors—elite behavior and the sociopolitical setting. Elite behavior refers to the attitude and practices of governmental and opposition elites concerning coalitions and decision-making. As Lijphart points out, there are coalescent and adversarial maneuvers. Based on our findings, a third form of elite behavior is distinguished—the accommodational:

1. Coalescent behavior occurs in political systems where, given the party system, there is an absolute need to create coalitions to form viable governments. Governmental policy-making rests exclusively in the hands of the coalitional partners who, in heterogeneous societies, represent the major segments of society;
2. Accommodational behavior occurs in democratic systems where, due to the party and electoral system, coalitions sometimes (but not always) need to be formed to create majority governments. Governmental decision-making often takes into account the views of otherwise non-governmental political elites;
3. Adversarial behavior may occur in a majoritarian political system where there are usually two major parties who vie for a winner-take all government. These parties never coalesce with one another as they do not need each other to rule or survive. Governmental decision-making remains, as well, exclusively in the hands of the governing party. Such adversarial behavior may also take place, however, in non-majoritarian systems where political polarization is deep and parties form one-sided ideological coalitions, one of which governs.

Based on this expanded view of elite behavior and the resulting new typology of democracies, it is possible to categorize the five cases profiled in this book (see Table 8.8):

1. The Federal Republic of West Germany is a centrist democracy. Set against a largely homogeneous/centripetal climate, the German

Table 8.8   A Typology of Democracies

		The Sociopolitical Picture	
		Homogeneous and Centripetal	Heterogeneous and/or Polarized
Political	Coalescent	DEPOLITICIZED* DEMOCRACY	CONSOCIATIONAL* DEMOCRACY
Elite	Accommo-dational	CENTRIST DEMOCRACY (Germany)	CONSENSUAL DEMOCRACY (Spain 1970s–80s Italy 1980s?)
Behavior	Adversarial	CENTRIPETAL* DEMOCRACY	CENTRIFUGAL* or POLARIZED DEMOCRACY (Spain 1930s, Italy & Portugal)

Note: *These designations are from Arend Lijphart's typology of democracies presented in Democracy in Plural Societies (New Haven: Yale University Press, 1977). This Table distinguishes a third form of elite behavior—the accommodational one—which helps to explain two additional types of democracy which do not neatly fit into Lijphart's scheme.

elites pursue largely accommodational decision-making strategies and often need a coalitional partner(s) to form a viable government.

2. Spain since 1979 has been a consensual democracy. It has displayed a continuation of accommodational elite behavior, evident in its consensual/compromise pattern of constitution-making, through both christian democratic and socialist governments. Coalitional partners have sometimes been needed for effective governing (namely under the UCD governments). Such accommodational behavior has survived in the face of problematic social heterogeneity (especially in the regions), difficult economic conditions and Spain's political semi-polarization.

3. Italy since World War Two can best be described as a polarized or centrifugal democracy although lately it seems to be evolving into a consensual form of democracy. Polarized democracies display adversarial elite practices over a backdrop of a heterogeneous and/or polarized sociopolitical climate. The governmental and political

Table 8.9 Possible Relationship Between the Type of Transition
and the Resulting Democratic Regime

Case Study	Type of Transition	Type of Regime
Spain 1930s	Polarized	Centrifugal
Germany 1940s	Unfettered	Centrist
Italy 1940s	Consensual	Centrifugal*
Portugal 1970s	Polarized	Centrifugal
Spain 1970s	Consensual	Consensual

Note: *Italy in the 1980s may be in the process of becoming a
consensual democracy as its major parties and political leaders seem
to be tending toward more accommodational, rather than adversarial,
behavior.

practices of the Spanish Second Republic and Portugal make these
cases of centrifugal democracy as well.

Is There a Relationship Between the Transition and the Resulting Democracy?

Although this is a difficult question to answer, it is tempting to
conclude trying. With the help of Table 8.9, some final observations
can be made. After its polarized transition, the Spanish Second Republic—a centrifugal democracy—was besent with a variety of socioeconomic, regional and religious conflicts, not to mention polarization.
Both the transition and the practices of the regime display the same
characteristics—political polarization, ideological coalitions and unilateral decision-making. The guideline quality of the constitution made
things worse as it allowed the implementation of highly dogmatic and
volatile measures—especially concerning the military and the Catholic
Church. Many of the trends evident during the transition not only
foretold the story of the Second Republic but also contributed to its
early demise.

In the German case an unfettered transition yielded a centrist democracy that to this day displays the prevalence of accommodational
behavior among its elites. Whether or not it is mere coincidence, there
is again a correspondence between the way in which politics were carried
out during Germany's transition to democracy and the way politics
have been practiced ever since. It is indisputable, moreover, that the

guideline quality of the Basic Law of 1949 has played a constructive role in the effective functioning of that regime.

In the case of post-war Italy, a centrifugal democracy has been more or less operative since the consensual transition of the late 1940s. The elite that carried out the transition displayed mostly consensual behavior, readily compromising on constitutional issues. The correspondence between the Italian type of transition and its form of democracy is not as great as that found in the two aforementioned cases. But it is still possible to find in the Italian transition seeds of the type of democracy that has existed there since—namely the polarized nature of its politics. It was only due to the pragmatic restraint of Italy's transitionary elites that a polarized or dissensual transition did not follow.

In Portugal a more predictable relationship, similar to that seen in the Spanish Second Republic, is evident—between a polarized transition and a resulting centrifugal democracy. Some major differences from the Spanish case, however, account for the continuing viability of the Portuguese model of democracy. Spain had an actively dissensual process while Portugal was only passively dissensual. The sociopolitical climate in Spain was far more divided, displaying not only political polarization but also various forms of social conflict. In Portugal, political polarization was the principal divisive factor. The Spanish Constitution of 1931 was a readily implementable dogmatic/guideline constitution while that in Portugal was dogmatic/ambiguous (and was subsequently revised in part). This brief comparison proves that even in cases that appear to be similar, different factors may have contributed to such eventual similarities. Only by doing so could one explain why the Spanish Second Republic succumbed to civil war after barely five years of existence while the Portuguese democracy has lasted over a decade.

Finally, in the recent Spanish case one witnesses the correspondence of a consensual transition and an emerging consensual democracy. The behavior of Spain's political elite during both the transition and within the democratic regime displays the continued practice of accommodational coalitions and decision-making patterns. This accommodational political behavior cannot be fitted into Lijphart's category of consociational democracy because in Spain governments are not formed by coalitions representing the major sociopolitical segments of society. What is more, Spain is not like Belgium where certain specific ethnic groups are aligned with particular political parties. In Spain one finds Basques voting as much for the PNV as they do for the PSOE. Accommodational behavior has kept Spain out of the ranks of centrifugal democracies for it has all the necessary conditions for such polarization. As long as such accommodational behavior continues to be the core of Spanish democracy its institutions and practices should become firmly footed.

One of the goals of this analysis has been to illustrate how total political change, under the proper conditions, is possible without violence. Most of the lessons learned have been based on an examination of both the process and the outcome of a transitionary constitution-making period. The ideological or multilateral character of the predominant coalition(s), the confrontational or accommodational nature of negotiations and the dogmatic or compromised, clear or ambiguous content of the resulting constitution tell us many things about the emerging regime. Within the transition to democracy, there is no better predictor of future political behavior than the analysis of constitution-making. Constitution-making is not only a microcosm of the larger political change that is unfolding and a major conduit for such change, it is also a laboratory in which one can begin to see the contours of future political behavior taking shape.

Notes

1. See generally, Gordon Wright, *The Reshaping of French Democracy* (Boston: Beacon Press, 1970).

2. Arend Lijphart, *Democracy in Plural Societies* (New Haven: Yale University Press, 1977).

Bibliography

ABC. Madrid: 1975–1980.

Adams, John Clarke and Paolo Barile. *The Government of Republican Italy*. New York: Houghton Mifflin Co., 1972.

Alba, Victor. *Transition in Spain: From Franco to Democracy*. New Brunswick, N.J.: Transaction Books, 1978.

Alba Navarro, Manuel. "El recurso previo de inconstitucionalidad contra proyectos de ley organica." *Revista de Derecho Politico*, No. 16, Winter 1982–83, 167–82.

Almagro Nosete, Jose. "Tutela procesal ordinaria y privilegiada (jurisdiccion constitucional) de los intereses difusos." *Revista de Derecho Politico*, No. 16, Winter 1982–83, 93–102.

―――. "La accion popular ante el Tribunal de Garantias Constitucionales. Valoracion critica." *Revista de Derecho Politico*, No. 12, Winter 1981–82, 65–83.

Alvarez, Santiago. "Spain at a Historic Crossroad." *World Marxist Review*, No. 19, June 1976, 72–80.

Alvarez Conde, Enrique. "La Constitucion española de 30 de junio de 1876: cuestiones previas." *Revista de Estudios Politicos*, No. 3, May-June 1978, 79–99.

Alzaga, Oscar. *La Constitucion española de 1978: comentario sistematico*. Madrid: Ediciones del Foro, 1978.

Amodia, Jose. *Franco's Political Legacy: From Dictatorship to Façade Democracy*. London: Allen Lane, Ltd., 1977.

Amsden, Jon. *Collective Bargaining and Class Conflict in Spain*. Trowbridge, England: Redwood Press, Ltd., 1972.

Anderson, Charles W. *The Political Economy of Modern Spain: Policy-making in an Authoritarian System*. Madison, Wisconsin: University of Wisconsin Press, 1970.

Aragon, Manuel. "El control de constitucionalidad en la Constitucion española de 1978." *Revista de Estudios Politicos*, No. 7, January-February 1979, 171–95.

Arango, E. Ramon. *The Spanish Political System: Franco's Legacy*. Boulder, Colorado: Westview Press, 1978.

Ariño Ortiz, Gaspar. "El control del gobierno sobre las empresas publicas en España." *International Review of Administrative Science*, XLVI, No. 1, 1980, 69–88.

Baklanoff, Eric N. *The Economic Transformation of Spain and Portugal*. New York: Praeger Publishers, 1978.

Bar, Antonio. "El problema del voto de desconfianza en la Constitucion española de 1931." *Revista de Derecho Politico*, No. 12, Winter 1981-82, 85-103.

Bassols Coma, Martin. "La planificacion economica en la Constitucion española de 1978." *International Review of Administrative Science*, XLVI, No. 1, 1980, 89-99.

Blackmer, Donald L.M., and Sidney Tarrow, eds. *Communism in Italy and France*. Princeton, N.J.: Princeton University Press, 1975.

Boletin Oficial de las Cortes, Congreso de Diputados. *Anteproyecto de Constitucion*. Madrid: Rivadeneyra, S. A., 17 April 1978.

Boletin Oficial del Estado. *Ley 1/1977 de 4 Enero para la Reforma Politica*. Madrid: Rivadeneyra, S. A., 5 January 1977.

Bonachela Mesas, Manuel. "Sobre el derrumbamiento de regimenes democraticos." *Revista de Estudios Politicos*, No. 9, May-June 1979, 121-36.

Bracher, Karl Dietrich. *The German Dictatorship*. New York: Praeger Publishers, 1970.

Braga de Macedo, Jorge and Simon Serfaty, eds. *Portugal since the Revolution: Economic and Political Perspectives*. Boulder, Colorado: Westview Press, 1981.

Brecht, Arnold. "The New German Constitution." *Social Research*, 16, No. 4, December 1949, 425-73.

Cambio 16. Madrid: 1978-1980.

Carothers, Thomas. "Spain, NATO and Democracy." *The World Today*, July-August 1981, 298-303.

Carrillo, Santiago. *Eurocommunism and the State*. Westport, Connecticut: Lawrence Hill & Co., 1978.

Cases Mendez, Jose Ignacio. "Resultados y abstencion en el Referendum español de 1978." *Revista de Estudios Politicos*, No. 6, November-December 1978, 175-204.

Chalmers, Douglas and Craig Robinson. "Why Power Contenders Choose Liberalization Perspectives from Latin America." Unpublished paper delivered at 1980 Annual Meeting of the American Political Science Association, Washington, D.C., August 1980.

Clark, Robert P. *The Basques: The Franco Years and Beyond*. Reno, Nevada: University of Nevada Press, 1979.

Claudin, Fernando. *Eurocommunism and Socialism*. London: New Left Books, 1978.

Colomer Viadel, Antonio. "El origen de la monarquia parlamentaria en España y el Anteproyecto Constitucional." *Revista de Estudios Politicos*. No. 3, May-June 1978, 101-20.

Committee on Foreign Relations, United States Senate. *Revolution into Democracy: Portugal after the Coup*. A Report by Senator George McGovern. Washington, D.C.: United States Printing Office, 1976.

Comyns Carr, R. "Will Spain's Development Plan Succeed?" *The World Today*, May 1963, 200-07.

Constitution of Greece. Athens: House of Parliament, 1975.

Constitution of the Portuguese Republic. Lisbon: Office of the Secretary of State for Mass Communications, Directorate General for Information and Diffusion, 1977.

Constitution of the Republic of Italy. Rome: Chamber of Deputies and Senate of the Republic, 1979.

Contreras, Manuel and Jose Ramon Montero. "Una Constitucion fragil: revisionismo y reforma constitucional en la II Republica española." *Revista de Derecho Politico,* No. 12, Winter 1981–82, 23–63.

Cortes: Diario de Sesiones del Congreso de los Diputados: Comision de Asuntos Constitucionales y Libertades Publicas. Madrid: Rivadeneyra, S. A., 5 May 1978–20 June 1978.

Cortes: Diario de Sesiones del Congreso de Diputados: Sesiones Plenarias. Madrid: Rivadeneyra, S. A., 4 July 1978 - 21 July 1978.

Cortes: Diario de Sesiones del Congreso de Diputados: Sesion Plenaria. Madrid: Rivadeneyra, S. A., 31 October 1978.

Cortes: Diario de Sesiones del Senado: Comision de Constitucion. Madrid: Rivadeneyra, S. A., 18 August 1978 - 14 September 1978.

Cortes: Diario de Sesiones del Senado: Sesiones Plenarias. Madrid: Rivadeneyra, S. A., 25 September 1978 - 5 October 1978.

Cortes: Diario de Sesiones del Senado: Sesion Plenaria. Madrid: Rivadeneyra, S. A., 31 October 1978.

Cortes: Diario de Sesiones: Sesion Conjunta del Congreso de los Diputados y del Senado. Madrid: Rivadeneyra, S. A., 27 December 1978.

Coverdale, John F. "Spain from Dictatorship to Democracy." *International Affairs* (London), 53, October 1977, 615–30.

————. *The Political Transformation of Spain after Franco.* New York: Praeger Publishers, 1979.

Dahl, Robert A. *Polyarchy.* New Haven, Connecticut: Yale University Press, 1971.

————, ed. *Regimes and Oppositions.* New Haven, Connecticut: Yale University Press, 1973.

De Blas Guerrero, Andres. "El Referendum Constitucional en el Pais Vasco." *Revista de Estudios Politicos,* No. 6, November-December 1978, 205–15.

De Cabo Martin, Carlos. "Estado y estado de derecho en el capitalismo dominante: aspectos significativos del planteamiento constitucional español." *Revista de Estudios Politicos,* No. 9, May-June 1979, 99–102.

De Esteban, Jorge and Luis Lopez Guerra et al. *El regimen constitucional español I.* Barcelona: Editorial Labor, 1980.

————. *El regimen constitucional español II.* Barcelona: Labor Universitaria, 1982.

De Vega Garcia, Pedro. "Jurisdiccion constitucional y crisis de la Constitucion." *Revista de Estudios Politicos,* No. 7, January-February 1979, 93–118.

Del Castillo Vera, Pilar. "La campaña del Referendum Constitucional." *Revista de Estudios Politicos,* No. 6, November-December 1978, 153–74.

Der Spiegel. Hamburg: 1980.

Edinger, Lewis J. *Politics in West Germany.* Boston: Little Brown & Co., 1977.

Ehrmann, Henry W. *Politics in France.* Boston: Little Brown & Co., 1976.

El Pais. Madrid: 1977–1980.

Elizalde, Jose. "Observaciones sobre el papel del Tribunal Constitucional en la delimitacion de competencias entre estado y comunidades autonomas." *Revista de Derecho Politico,* No. 16, Winter 1982–83, 143–66.

Estudios sobre el Proyecto de Constitucion. Madrid: Centro de Estudios Constitucionales, 1978.

Fernandez Segado, Francisco. "La suspension de garantias constitucionales en la nueva Constitucion española." *Revista de Estudios Politicos,* No. 7, January-February 1979, 299–312.

Fields, Rona M. *The Portuguese Revolution and the Armed Forces Movement.* New York: Praeger Publishers, 1976.

Fierro Bardaji, Alfred. "Political Positions and Opposition in the Spanish Catholic Church." *Government and Opposition,* 11, No. 2, September 1976, 198–211.

Finer, S. E., ed. *Five Constitutions.* Sussex, New Jersey: The Harvester Press-Humanities Press, 1979.

Fraga Iribarne, Manuel. *Ideas para la reconstruccion de una España con futuro.* Barcelona: Editorial Planeta, 1980.

———. *La Monarquia y el pais.* Barcelona: Editorial Planeta, 1977.

Fraser, Ronald. "Spain on the Brink." *New Left Review,* March-April 1976, 3–33.

Friederich, Carl J. *Constitutional Government and Democracy: Theory and Practice in Europe and America.* Boston: Little Brown & Co., 1941.

———. *Limited Government: A Comparison.* Englewood Cliffs, New Jersey: Prentice Hall, 1974.

Galeotti, Sergio and Bruno Rossi. "El Tribunal Constitucional en la nueva Constitucion española: medios de impugnacion y legitimados para actuar." *Revista de Estudios Politicos,* No. 7, January-February 1979, 119–43.

Gallagher, Tom. "The Growing Pains of Portuguese Democracy." *The World Today,* March 1981, 102–09.

Garcia-Atance, Maria Victoria. "Cronica parlamentaria sobre la Constitucion española de 1931." *Revista de Derecho Politico,* No. 12, Winter 1981–82, 295–306.

Garcia Cotarelo, Ramon. "Notas sobre el Anteproyecto de Constitucion." *Revista de Estudios Politicos,* No. 1, January-February 1978, 133–41.

Garcia Herrera, Miguel Angel. "La Comision Mixta Congreso-Senado." *Revista de Estudios Politicos,* No. 4, July-August 1978, 67–95.

Garrido Falla, Fernando. "La institucion administrativa de la Constitucion española." *International Review of Administrative Science,* XLVI, No. 1, 1980, 1–8.

Garrorena Morales, Angel. *Autoritarismo y control parlamentario en las Cortes de Franco.* Murcia: Publicaciones del Departamento de Derecho Politico, 1977.

Gati, Charles. "The 'Europeanization' of Communism?" *Foreign Affairs,* 88, No. 3, April 1977, 539–53.

Gay, Peter. *Weimar Culture.* New York: Harper & Row, 1968.

Gilbert, Felix. *The End of the European Era: 1890 to the Present.* New York: W. W. Norton Co., 1970.

Goldborough, James. "Eurocommunism after Madrid." *Foreign Affairs,* 55, No. 4, July 1977, 800–14.

Gomez Reina y Carnota, Enrique. "La libertad de expresion en la II Republica." *Revista de Derecho Politico,* No. 12, Winter 1981–82, 159–87.

Gonzalez, Felipe and Alfonso Guerra. *Partido Socialista Obrero Español.* Bilbao: Ediciones Albia, 1977.

Graham, Lawrence S. *Portugal: The Decline and Collapse of an Authoritarian Order.* London and Beverly Hills: Sage Publications, 1975.

Graham, L. S. and H. M. Makler, eds. *Contemporary Portugal: The Revolution and its Antecedents.* Austin, Texas: University of Texas Press, 1979.

Guaita, Aurelio. "El recurso de amparo contra tribunales." *Revista de Derecho Politico,* No. 16, Winter 1982–83, 65–91.

––––––. "Las regiones en la Constitucion española de 1978." *International Review of Administrative Science,* XLV, No. 2, 1979, 147–55.

Gunther, Richard and Roger A. Blough. "Religious Conflict and Consensus in Spain: A Tale of Two Constitutions." *World Affairs,* 143, No. 4, Spring 1981, 366–412.

Harsgor, Michael. *Portugal in Revolution.* Beverly Hills, California: Sage Publications, Washington Paper No. 32, 1976.

Hermet, Guy. "Spain under Franco: The Changing Character of the Authoritarian Regime." *European Journal of Political Research,* No. 4, 1976, 311–27.

Hernandez Gil, Antonio. *El cambio politico español y la Constitucion.* Barcelona: Editorial Planeta, 1982.

Herrero de Miñon, Miguel. "Falsas y verdaderas vias del consenso constitucional." *Revista de Estudios Politicos,* No. 9, May-June 1979, 73–97.

Heubel, E. J. "Church and State in Spain: Transition toward Independence and Liberty." *Western Political Quarterly,* 29, No. 4, December 1976, 125–39.

Hottinger, Arnold. "Spain on the Road to Democracy." *The World Today,* 33, September 1977, 353–62.

––––––. "Spain One Year after Franco." *The World Today,* 32, December 1976, 441–50.

Huntington, Samuel. *Political Order in Changing Societies.* New Haven, Connecticut: Yale University Press, 1967.

–––––– and Clement Moore, eds. *Authoritarian Politics in Modern Society.* New York: Basic Books, 1970.

Kamynin, L. "A Panorama of Spain Today." *International Affairs (Moscow),* April 1979, 30–8.

Laboa, Juan Maria. *Iglesia y religion en las constituciones españolas.* Madrid: Ediciones Encuentro, 1981.

Lancaster, Thomas D. and Gary Prevost, eds. *Politics and Change in Spain.* New York: Praeger Publishers, 1985.

Lepsius, Rainer. "From Fragmented Party Democracy to Government by Emergency Decree." In *The Breakdown of Democratic Regimes: Europe,* Juan J. Linz and Alfred Stepan, eds. Baltimore, Maryland: The Johns Hopkins University Press, 1978, 34–79.

Levine, Robert M. "Brazil: The Dimensions of Democratization." *Current History*, 81, No. 472, Fall 1982, 60–3 ff.

Lijphart, Arend. *Democracy in Plural Societies*. New Haven, Connecticut: Yale University Press, 1977.

———. *The Politics of Accommodation: Pluralism and Democracy in the Netherlands*. Berkeley, California: University of California Press, 1975.

Linde Paniagua, Enrique and Miguel Herrero Lera. "El Referendum: de las Leyes Fundamentales al Anteproyecto de Constitucion." *Revista de Estudios Politicos*, No. 2, March-April 1978, 87–106.

Linz, Juan J. "An Authoritarian Regime: Spain." In *Mass Politics*, Erik Allardt and Stein Rokkan, eds. New York: Free Press, 1970, 251–83.

———. "Europe's Southern Frontier: Evolving Trends toward What?" *Daedalus*, 1979, 175–210.

———. "From Falange to Movimiento-Organizacion: The Spanish Single Party and the Franco Regime, 1936–1968." In *Authoritarian Politics in Modern Society*, Samuel Huntington and Clement Moore, eds. New York: Basic Books, 1970, 128–201.

———. "From Great Hopes to Civil War: The Breakdown of Democracy in Spain." In *The Breakdown of Democratic Regimes: Europe*, Juan J. Linz and Alfred Stepan, eds. Baltimore, Maryland: The Johns Hopkins University Press, 1978, 142–215.

———. "Legislatures in Organic Statist-Authoritarian Regimes—The Case of Spain." In *Legislatures in Development: Dynamics of Change in New and Old States*, Joel Smith and Lloyd D. Musolf, eds. Durham, North Carolina: Duke University Press, 1979.

———. "Opposition to and under an Authoritarian Regime." In *Regimes and Oppositions*, Robert A. Dahl, ed. New Haven, Connecticut: Yale University Press, 1973, 171–259.

———. "Spain and Portugal: Critical Choices." In *Western Europe: The Trials of Partnership*, David S. Landes, ed. Lexington, Massachusetts: Lexington Books, 1977, 237–96.

———. "The Future of an Authoritarian Situation." In *Authoritarian Brazil*, Alfred Stepan, ed. New Haven, Connecticut: Yale University Press, 1973.

———. "The Spanish Party System." Paper delivered at Ninth World Congress of Sociology, Committee of Political Sociology, Uppsala, Sweden, August 15, 1978.

———. "Totalitarian and Authoritarian Regimes." In *Handbook of Political Science*, Volume III, Fred Greenstein and Nelson Polsby, eds. Reading, Massachusetts: Addison Wesley, 1975, 175–412.

———, Manuel Gomez-Reino, Francisco A. Orizo and Dario Vila. *Informe sociologico sobre el cambio politico en España 1975/1981*. Madrid: Fundacion FOESSA, Editorial Euramerica, S.A., 1981.

——— and Alfred Stepan, eds. *The Breakdown of Democratic Regimes*. Four Volumes. Baltimore, Maryland: The Johns Hopkins Press, 1978.

Lopez-Pintor, Rafael. "Transition toward Democracy in Spain: Opinion Mood and Elite Behavior." Paper delivered at Conference on Prospects for Democracy: Transitions from Authoritarian Rule in Latin America and Latin Europe, Wilson International Center for Scholars, Smithsonian Institution, Washington, D. C., October 1980.

Loewenstein, Karl. "Reflection on the Value of Constitutions in our Revolutionary Age." In *Constitutions and Constitutional Trends since World War II*, Arnold J. Zurcher, ed. New York: New York University Press, 1951, 191–224.

Lopez Rodo, Laureano. "Las autonomias en la nueva Constitucion española." *International Review of Administrative Science*, XLVI, No. 2, 1980, 146 ff.

Lucas Murillo, Pablo and Roberto Toniatti. "Seminario sobre el Proyecto de Constitucion español." *Revista de Estudios Politicos*, No. 4, July-August 1978, 181–91.

Lucas Verdu, Pablo. *La Octava Ley Fundamental: critica juridico-politica de la reforma Suarez*. Madrid: Editorial Tecnos, 1976.

———. "La singularidad del proceso constituyente español." *Revista de Estudios Politicos*, No. 1, January-February 1978, 9–27.

McInnes, Neil. *Eurocommunism*. Beverly Hills, California: Sage Publications, Washington Paper No. 37, 1976.

McRae, Kenneth, ed. *Consociational Democracy: Political Accommodation in Segmented Societies*. Toronto: McClelland & Stewart Ltd., 1974.

Maier, Lothar. *Spaniens Weg Zur Demokratie*. Meisenheim am Glan, West Germany: Verlag Anton Hain, 1977.

Malloy, James M., ed. *Authoritarianism and Corporatism in Latin America*. Pittsburgh, Pennsylvania: University of Pittsburgh Press, 1974.

Maravall, J. M. "Modernization, Authoritarianism and the Growth of Working Class Dissent: The Case of Spain." *Government and Opposition*, 8, April 1973, 432–54.

———. "Political Cleavages in Spain and the 1979 Elections." *Government and Opposition*, 14, No. 3, Summer 1979, 299–317.

———. "Students and Politics in Contemporary Spain." *Government and Opposition*, 11, No. 2, Spring 1976, 156–79.

———. "Transition to Democracy, Political Alignments and Elections in Spain." Paper delivered at Conference on Prospects for Democracy: Transitions from Authoritarian Rule in Latin America and Latin Europe, Wilson International Center for Scholars, Smithsonian Institution, Washington, D. C., October 1980.

Martin, Edwin M. "Haiti: A Case Study in Futility." *SAIS Review*, 2, Summer 1981, 61–70.

Maxwell, Kenneth, ed. *The Press and the Rebirth of Iberian Democracy*. Westport, Connecticut: Greenwood Press, 1983.

———. "The Thorns of the Portuguese Revolution." *Foreign Affairs*, 54, January 1976, 250–70.

Medhurst, Kenneth. "The Military and the Prospects for Spanish Democracy." *West European Politics*, 1, No. 1, February 1978, 42–59.

———. "The Prospects of Federalism: The Regional Problem after Franco." *Government and Opposition*, 11, No. 2, Spring 1976, 180–97.

Medina, Manuel. "Spain in Europe." *Government and Opposition*, 11, No. 2, Spring 1976, 143–55.

Medvedenko, A. "The Ultras turn to Terror." *New Times* (Moscow), No. 6, February 1977, 8–9.

Meisler, Stanley. "Spain's New Democracy." *Foreign Affairs*, 56, October 1977, 190–208.

Menges, Constantine. "Deepening Shadows over a Fragile Democracy." *Worldview*, 21, April 1978, 14–18.

———. *Spain: The Struggle for Democracy*. Beverly Hills, California: Sage Publications, Washington Paper No. 58, 1978.

Merkl, Peter. *The Origin of the West German Republic*. New York: Oxford University Press, 1963.

Middlebrook, Kevin J. "Notes on Transitions from Authoritarian Rule in Latin America and Latin Europe: A Rapporteur's Report." Paper delivered at Conference on Prospects for Democracy: Transitions from Authoritarian Rule in Latin America and Latin Europe, Wilson International Center for Scholars, Smithsonian Institution, Washington, D. C., October 1980.

Montero Puerto, Miguel. "La alternativa defensor del pueblo—Ministerio Fiscal en la garantia jurisdiccional de derechos fundamentales and libertades publicas en España." *International Review of Administrative Science*, XLVI, No. 1, 1980, 48–60.

Mouzelis, Nicos. "Regime Instability and the State in Peripheral Capitalism: A General Theory and Case Study of Greece." Paper delivered at Conference on Prospects for Democracy: Transitions from Authoritarian Rule in Latin America and Latin Europe, Wilson International Center for Scholars, Smithsonian Institution, Washington, D. C., October 1980.

Mujal-Leon, Eusebio. "The PCE in Spanish Politics." *Problems of Communism*, 27, July-August 1978, 15–37.

Naylon, John. *Andalusia*. New York: Oxford University Press, 1975.

Nordlinger, Eric A. *Conflict Regulation in Divided Societies*. Cambridge, Massachusetts: Center for International Affairs, Harvard University, Occasional Paper in International Affairs No. 29, 1972.

Nwabueze, B. O. *Constitutionalism in Emergent States*. London: C. Hurst & Co., 1973.

O'Donnell, Guillermo. *Modernization and Bureaucratic Authoritarianism*. Berkeley, California: University of Berkeley Press, 1973.

Ortiz, Pauline. "The Spanish Right is Organizing." *Labour Monthly*, 61, No. 1, January 1979, 22–27.

Overholt, William, ed. *The Future of Brazil*. Boulder, Colorado: Westview Press, 1978.

Payne, Stanley. "In the Twilight of the Franco Years." *Foreign Affairs*, 49, January 1971, 342–54.

———. "Terror and Democratic Stability in Spain." *Current History*, 77, No. 451, November 1979, 167–71 ff.

———. *The History of Spain and Portugal*. Two Volumes. Madison, Wisconsin: University of Wisconsin Press, 1973.

———. "The Political Transformation of Spain." *Current History*, 73, No. 431, November 1977, 165–68 ff.

Peces-Barba, Gregorio and Luis Prieto Sanchis. *La Constitucion española de 1978: un estudio de derecho y politica.* Valencia: Fernando Torres—Editor, S. A., 1981.

Penniman, Howard R., ed. *Greece at the Polls: The National Elections of 1974 and 1977.* Washington, D. C.: American Enterprise Institute, 1981.

Perez Luño, Antonio Enrique. "La proteccion de la intimidad frente a la informatica en la Constitucion española de 1978." *Revista de Estudios Politicos,* No. 9, May-June 1979, 59–72.

Predieri, Alberto and E. Garcia de Enterria. *La Constitucion española de 1978: estudio sistematico.* Madrid: Editorial Civitas, 1981.

Preston, Paul. "The Dilemma of Credibility: The Spanish Communist Party, the Franco Regime and After." *Government and Opposition,* 11, Winter 1976, 65–83.

———. "The Spanish Constitutional Referendum of 6 December 1978." *West European Politics,* 2, No. 2, May 1979, 246–49.

Revel, Jean-Francois. "Spain's Prospects Brighten: A Surprising Monarch Proves Politically Deft." *Atlas,* 23, October 1976, 42–43.

———. "The Myths of Eurocommunism." *Foreign Affairs,* 56, No. 2, January 1978, 295–305.

———. *The Totalitarian Temptation.* Garden City, New York: Doubleday & Co., Inc., 1977.

Robinson, Richard. *Contemporary Portugal: A History.* London: George Allen & Unwin, 1979.

Roman, Manuel. *The Limits of Economic Growth in Spain.* New York: Praeger Publishers, 1971.

Roman, Paloma and Francisco J. Vanaclocha. "Repertorio bibliografico sobre aspectos juridico-politicos e institucionales de la Segunda Republica española." *Revista de Derecho Politico,* No. 12, Winter 1981–82, 399–415.

Romero, Cesar Enrique. "Constitucion y cambio sociopolitico." *Revista de Estudios Politicos,* No. 205, January-February 1976, 223–34.

Romero Maura, Joaquin. "After Franco, Franquismo?: The Armed Forces, the Crown and Democracy." *Government and Opposition,* 11, Winter 1976, 35–64.

Roskin, Michael. "Spain Tries Democracy Again." *Political Science Quarterly,* 93, Winter 1978–79, 629–46.

Rubio Llorente, Francisco. "Del Tribunal de Garantias al Tribunal Constitucional." *Revista de Derecho Politico,* No. 16, Winter 1982–83, 27–37.

——— and Manuel Aragon Reyes. "Enunciados, aparentemente vacios, en la regulacion constitucional del control de la constitucionalidad." *Revista de Estudios Politicos,* No. 7, January-February 1979, 161–69.

Ruiz Lapeña, Rosa Maria. "El recurso de amparo durante la II Republica española." *Revista de Estudios Politicos,* No. 7, January-February 1979, 291–98.

Rustow, Dankwart. "Transitions to Democracy: A Dynamic Model." *Comparative Politics,* April 1970, 337–63.

Salisbury, William T. and James D. Theberge. *Spain in the 1970s: Economics, Social Structure, Foreign Policy.* New York: Praeger Publishers, 1976.

Sanchez Agesta, Luis. *Ley electoral.* Madrid: Editorial Revista de Derecho Privado, 1977.

Sanchez Gonzalez, Santiago. "La competencia del Tribunal Constitucional en materia de conflictos: una breve nota sobre una cuestion conflictiva." *Revista de Derecho Politico,* No. 16, Winter 1982-83, 193-200.

Sartori, Giovanni. "Constitutionalism: A Preliminary Discussion." *American Political Science Review,* LVI, No. 4, December 1962, 853-64.

――――. *Democratic Theory.* New York: Praeger Publishers, 1967.

――――. *Parties and Party Systems.* Volume 1. Cambridge, Massachusetts: Cambridge University Press, 1976.

――――. "Political Development and Political Engineering." In *Public Policy,* John D. Montgomery and Albert O. Hirschman, eds. Cambridge, Massachusetts: Harvard University Press, 1968, 261-98.

Schmitter, Philippe C. *Interest, Conflict and Political Change in Brazil.* Stanford, California: Stanford University Press, 1971.

――――. "Still the Century of Corporatism?" *Review of Politics,* 36, No. 1, January 1974, 85-131.

Schwartz, Pedro. "Politics First: The Economy after Franco." *Government and Opposition,* 11, Winter 1976, 84-103.

Silva Muñoz, Federico. *La transicion inacabada.* Barcelona: Editorial Planeta, 1980.

Singh, M. M. *The Constitution of India: Studies in Perspective.* Calcutta: The World Press Private Ltd., 1975.

Smith, Joel and Lloyd D. Musolf, eds. *Legislatures in Development: Dynamics of Change in New and Old States.* Durham, North Carolina: Duke University Press, 1979.

Spanish Constitution 1978. Madrid: Ministerio de Asuntos Exteriores, Oficina de Informacion Diplomatica, 1979.

Soler Fando, Francisco. *Eurocomunismo y España.* Valencia: Editorial Prometeo, 1978.

Stepan, Alfred, ed. *Authoritarian Brazil.* New Haven, Connecticut: Yale University Press, 1973.

――――. *The Military in Politics: Changing Patterns in Brazil.* Princeton, New Jersey: Princeton University Press, 1971.

Stewart, Gaither. "Andalusia's Challenge to Spain." *The World Today,* May 1981, 194-200.

Story, Jonathan. "Spanish Political Parties: Before and After the Elections." *Government and Opposition,* 12, Autumn 1977, 474-95.

Tamames, Ramon. *Adonde vas España?* Barcelona: Editorial Planeta, 1976.

Tello Lazaro, Jose Angel. "Constitucion legal y constitucion real en el estado español de los siglos XIX y XX." *Revista de Estudios Politicos,* No. 2, March-April 1978, 193-97.

The Economist. London: 1977-1983.

The New York Times. New York: 1974-1983.

The Wall Street Journal. New York: 1979-1982.

Thouez, Jean Pierre. "Apprenticeship in Democracy with Spain's 'Civilized' Right." *International Perspectives,* September-October 1977, 35-40.

Time Magazine. New York: 1975–1983.

Tomas y Valiente, Francisco. "La defensa de la Constitucion." *Revista de Derecho Politico*, No. 16, Winter 1982–83, 185–92.

Trujillo, Gumersindo. "Juicio de legitimidad e interpretacion constitucional: cuestiones problematicas en el horizonte constitucional español." *Revista de Estudios Politicos*, No. 7, January-February 1979, 145–59.

Tusell Gomez, Javier et al. "Las constituyentes de 1931: unas elecciones de transicion." *Revista de Derecho Politico*, No. 12, Winter 1981–82, 189–270.

Vatikiotis, J. *Greece: A Political Essay.* Beverly Hills, California: Sage Publications, Washington Paper No. 11, 1974.

Vilar, Sergio. *Carta abierta a la oposicion.* Barcelona: Editorial Planeta, 1977.

Villarroya, Joaquin Tomas. "Proceso constituyente y nueva constitucion: un analisis critico." *Revista de Estudios Politicos*, No. 10, July-August 1979, 59–85.

Walker, Thomas W. *Nicaragua: A Profile of the Land of Sandino.* Boulder, Colorado: Westview Press, 1981.

———, ed. *Nicaragua in Revolution.* New York: Praeger Publishers, 1981.

Wright, Gordon. *The Reshaping of French Democracy.* Boston: Beacon Press, 1970.

Zapirain, Santiago. "A Turning Point in the Struggle for Democracy in Spain." *World Marxist Review*, 19, October 1976, 59–64.

Zariski, Raphael. *Italy: The Politics of Uneven Development.* Hinsdale, Illinois: The Dryden Press, Inc., 1972.

Zurcher, Arnold J., ed. *Constitutions and Constitutional Trends since World War II.* New York: New York University Press, 1951.

Index